I0120257

Congregational Society

The Wellesley Cook Book

Congregational Society

The Wellesley Cook Book

ISBN/EAN: 9783744785082

Printed in Europe, USA, Canada, Australia, Japan

Cover: Foto ©Andreas Hilbeck / pixelio.de

More available books at **www.hansebooks.com**

THE

WELLESLEY COOK BOOK

PREPARED BY THE

LADIES OF THE CONGREGATIONAL SOCIETY

———

BOSTON

C. J. PETERS & SON

1890

COPYRIGHT, 1890,

BY I. A. SANBORN.

PREFACE

THIS book was prepared by the Parlor Fund Committee, to aid in building the contemplated additions to the church, and has been made from a collection of receipts donated by the ladies of Wellesley. They are not original but favorite rules chosen by those whose names are given as guarantees of excellence. Advertisements have been solicited to pay the expenses of publication, but in no case have any been received from parties whose goods our ladies have not themselves tested and can cordially recommend.

Books may be ordered by mail from each of the committee.

> MRS. BENJ. H. SANBORN,
> MRS. ALBERT JENNINGS,
> MRS. H. E. CURRIER,
> ELIZABETH R. HORR,
> MRS. T. B. ROLLINS,
> *Parlor Fund Committee.*

WELLESLEY, MASS., June, 1890.

NOTE.— Blank pages are left in this book for writing in other receipts or making changes.

1

CONTENTS

http:/

THE
Hicks Brown Company
MERCHANT MILLERS,
MANSFIELD, OHIO, U.S.A.

THE flour made by this Company, having been thoroughly tested in actual use by the authors of this Cook Book, has justly entitled them to the space given them for advertising.

The celebrated brands of flour made by this Company are well known throughout New England for their purity, uniformity, and the general good qualities of a strictly pure "Winter Wheat" flour, and are far superior to any "Spring" flour for domestic use. A trial of their brands will satisfy any one as to their superiority.

THESE BRANDS ARE:

"HUNGARIAN," 1st Patent;
"BROWN'S BEST," 2d Patent;
"DAYLIGHT," Straight;
"WINTER KING," Clear.

This Company also makes "Graham" flour, which, like all of their other flour, stands pre-eminently in the front as an article of healthy nutrition.

For further particulars, address

THE HICKS BROWN COMPANY, Mansfield, Ohio.

WELLESLEY COOK BOOK

BREAD

As bread is the staff of life, be ye careful that it is sound and light.

WHEAT BREAD

PARE three moderately large mealy potatoes, cut them into slices three-fourths of an inch thick, and boil them in a small covered dish with a little water and salt. When the potatoes are well cooked, pour off the water, sift them through a small strainer, stir in flour and water enough to make a quart or more of rather stiff batter, add a cake of compressed yeast, and set in a warm place. The batter will rise in one hour. Mix four quarts of flour, one-half cup of lard rubbed into the flour, one tablespoonful of sugar, salt, and the yeast so as to form a very stiff dough.

The sponge will be ready to knead in three hours, and may be shaped into four loaves. Bread made in this way is always sweet and very light. The dough must not be allowed to stand over night, as it rises too quickly.

Mrs E. A. Jennings.

WHEAT BREAD

DRY in the oven over night three quarts of flour. The secret of good bread depends upon having the flour very dry and the yeast fresh.

Make a sponge early in the morning with one cup of

3

flour, one cup of warm milk and a cake of compressed yeast. Let it rise until it begins to fall.

Mix the three quarts of dried flour with three pints of warm milk, or water, a tablespoonful each of sugar, lard, and salt. When well mixed, add the sponge and work the mixture ten minutes. Let it rise till half as high again as at first.

Mould or knead it ten minutes more, and let it rise till twice its original height. Mould into loaves or biscuit, and when moderately light bake in a slow oven.

M. H. L.

BREAD

1 pint of milk	1 tablespoonful butter
1-2 pint cold water	1 tablespoonful sugar
1-2 cake of Fleischmann's yeast dissolved in cold water	1 teaspoonful salt, all dissolved in 1-2 pint HOT water

ADD to the milk and cold water in the mixing-bowl the solution of the butter, sugar, and salt, and the solution of the yeast. Stir in flour enough to make a not very stiff batter. Do *not* knead it, but mix it with a knife, cutting it through, and working it over until all the dry flour is well mixed with the other materials. Scrape the dough from the sides of the mixing-dish, smooth the top with a knife. Cover with a thick cloth, and let the batter rise. Shape into loaves; and when sponge has well risen, bake about forty minutes. Makes four good-sized loaves.

The Eliot.

BREAD WITH WHOLE WHEAT FLOUR

1 quart tepid water	1 teaspoonful salt
1 tablespoonful butter	1-2 yeast cake
1 tablespoonful sugar	Flour enough to make a stiff batter

MIX over night or in the morning. Keep at a temperate degree of heat. When light, stir down, remove to moulding-board. Work in only enough flour to allow the forming into loaves. Place in pans. Let it rise again, and bake in a quick but not too hot oven.

In preparing the bread for the pans, mould as little as possible. The above rule makes two loaves.

Mrs. Nathan Abbott.

WHOLE WHEAT FLOUR BREAD

SOAK half a cake of Warner's Safe Yeast in one quart of lukewarm water, with salt. With the sifted whole wheat, use one coffee cup of sifted white flour. Use enough flour to make a batter that will drop thickly from the spoon. Set over night in warm room. In the morning, pour into bread pans, two-thirds full. Let it rise to top. Good oven.

Mrs. Clements.

GRAHAM BREAD

ONE pint of warm milk, or milk and water, half of a yeast cake (compressed), and flour enough to make a *thin batter.* Let this rise over night, and in the morning stir in half a cup of sugar, a little salt, one teaspoonful of saleratus dissolved in water, and Graham (Arlington meal) enough to make a *stiff batter.* All the other ingredients should be thoroughly beaten into the sponge before adding the Graham, which should be stirred in a *little at a time,* and *beaten well.* Cut into biscuit, or shape into loaves, as preferred, and place in the baking-pans. Let it rise until very light, an hour and a half, or two hours, and bake. The oven should not be so hot as for white bread.

Do not make it too stiff.

M. Brown.

GRAHAM BREAD

1 pint Graham flour	2 teaspoonfuls Royal Bak-
1 pint wheat flour	ing Powder
1 1-2 pints milk	1 egg
1-2 cup sugar	

SIFT flour, salt, powder; add sugar, egg, and milk; bake with good oven.

A. M. C.

GRAHAM BREAD

THREE and three-quarters cups of warm water, one-third of a yeast cake, very little salt, a small cup molasses, one large quart Graham, one large quart St. Louis flour. If not quite stiff enough, always add flour rather than Graham.

Mrs. Stoddard.

GRAHAM BREAD

1 quart warm water	Scant half-pint molasses
2 quarts flour	A little salt
1 3-4 quarts Graham flour	1-2 yeast cake

LET it rise over night.

Mrs. N. H. Dadmun.

RYE BREAD

2 cups rye meal	Yeast powder, or 1 teaspoon-
1 heaping cup flour	ful of soda and 2 of cream
1 egg	of tartar
2 tablespoonfuls molasses	

MIX with milk, or milk and water, to pour easily from a spoon. Bake in gem pans or in a loaf.

E. Marietta Dewing.

BROWN BREAD

1 pint rye meal	1 pint wheat flour
1 pint bolted Indian meal	2-3 cup molasses
2-3 cup yeast	

SCALD the Indian meal, and when cool add the other ingredients. Moisten with sweet skimmed milk. Mix thoroughly and put into a tin pail with a close-fitting cover. Let it stand two hours; then set it in the oven, on two bricks. Let the temperature of the oven for the first half-hour be of the degree required to bake apple pies; then keep a *very slow* fire for five or six hours.

Mrs. E. A. Jennings.

BOSTON BROWN BREAD

2 cups sour milk
2 cups Indian meal
1 cup molasses
1 cup rye or Graham flour

1 1-2 teaspoonfuls of soda sifted
with 1-3 cup white flour
1 teaspoonful salt

Mix molasses and sour milk, then stir in the meal and flour. Pour into a buttered pail and steam three hours, then set in the oven and bake from twenty to thirty minutes.

Winifred E. Badger.

STEAMED BROWN BREAD

1 cup Indian meal
2 cups rye meal
2-3 cup molasses

1-2 teaspoonful soda
1-2 teaspoonful salt

Wet with milk or water. Stir well together. Steam three hours.

Mrs. Hobart.

STEAMED BROWN BREAD

Two cups Indian meal, two cups rye meal, one cup flour, one teaspoonful salt, mixed; one small cup molasses, one and one-half pints milk and water (half and half), or the same quantity sour milk, one heaping teaspoonful soda. Steam three hours.

Mrs. Stoddard.

BROWN BREAD

1 cup Indian meal
1 cup flour
2 1-3 cups rye meal
2 teaspoonfuls salt

cup molasses
1-2 teaspoonfuls soda
1-2 pints milk

Dissolve soda in a little boiling water and stir into the molasses. Steam six or seven hours.

Miss Hall.

CORN BREAD

1 pint of white Indian meal (full)	2 1-2 teaspoonfuls of Royal Baking Powder
1 teacup wheat flour	Milk
3 eggs	Butter the size of a walnut
3 tablespoonfuls sugar (scant)	

SIFT the meal, flour, sugar, and baking powder together through a flour sieve; work through the mixture the butter, add the eggs well beaten, and enough milk to cause the batter to just begin to pour from the spoon instead of dropping. Bake in gem pans.

M. H. L.

BROWN BREAD

2 cupfuls Indian meal	3 cupfuls sour milk or water
2 cupfuls coarse flour	1 teaspoonful soda
1 cupful molasses	

STEAM three hours and bake one-half hour.

Mrs. Mary L. Whipple.

STEAMED BROWN BREAD

1 1-2 cups Indian meal	1-2 cup molasses
1 1-2 cups rye meal	1 teaspoonful soda
2-3 cup flour	Salt

MIX soft with cold water, and boil three hours.

Lucy T. Winsor.

POTATO YEAST

12 potatoes	1 tablespoonful salt
1 quart boiling water	1 tablespoonful sugar
1 quart cold water	1 cup baker's yeast (or raise
1 tablespoonful flour	with cake yeast)

BOIL and mash the potatoes, and put them through a hair sieve, add the flour and then the cold water; then the boiling water, salt, and sugar. When sufficiently cool, put in the yeast, and set it to rise. Bottle the next day.

H. E. C.

SPANISH BUNNS

1 lb. flour	3 eggs
1-2 lb. sugar	1 cup fresh yeast
1-4 lb. butter	A little mace

MILK to make it the consistency of pound cake; beat well together, and put it in the tin you intend baking in. Set in a warm place, and bake like loaf bread, when light.

Mrs. H. F. Durant.

CINNAMON BUNNS

ONE pint of risen white dough. Work into this two well-beaten eggs, one-half cup of brown sugar, and one-fourth of a cup of melted butter, and enough flour to roll it into a sheet fourteen inches in length by ten in width and about one-half inch in thickness. Sprinkle this sheet of dough generously with brown sugar and pow-dered cinnamon, and roll it into a tight roll as you do a sponge roll. Then slice it down with a sharp knife into rolls one-half inch thick and set these to rise in a greased pan till light, when they may be baked as biscuit.

One-half cup of seedless raisins may be stirred into the dough if desired.

Mrs. Cowan.

BUNNS

3 eggs	3 cups milk
2 cups sugar	2-3 cup yeast
1-2 cup butter	Teaspoonful soda

USE the eggs, sugar and milk and flour to make a sponge. In the morning melt the butter and add with all the flour you can stir in with a spoon. In summer, when light, set the dough in a cool place till about two o'clock, then roll out, cut, fold over, and put in pans to rise. After baking rub over with sugar and water, or the white of an egg.

Mrs. Bacon.

BUNNS

3 cups new milk	1 cup butter
2 cups sugar	1 cup dried currants
1 cup yeast	

TAKE three cups of milk, one cup of sugar, one cup of yeast, and flour enough to make a stiff batter. After it rises, add one cup of sugar, one cup of butter, and knead it and let it rise again; cut it into cakes and let it rise again very light after putting into the pans. Add nutmeg if you like. Brush over the top with the white of egg and molasses when you take from oven.

M. Brown.

ROLLS

BOIL one pint milk, put in one large tablespoonful of butter while it cools; mix one large tablespoonful of sugar with three pints of flour, and a little salt, and one teacup of baker's yeast, or make a cup of yeast by taking two-thirds of a yeast cake dissolved in one-half cup of warm water, and flour enough for a thin batter. Let this rise for an hour before mixing the rolls. This should give the teacupful of yeast.

Mrs. Stoddard.

RUSK

4 lbs. flour	3-4 lb. butter
1 lb. sugar	1 pint milk
4 eggs	Cinnamon
Yeast	

RUB flour and butter together; add sugar. Set a sponge with the milk and yeast. In the morning add the beaten eggs, make into three loaves and let it rise. Bake one hour in a slow oven — a little over-doing injures it greatly.

Mrs. Bacon.

RUSK

1 cup sugar	1-3 cup butter
1 egg	1 teaspoonful soda
1 cup sour milk	1-2 teaspoonful each cloves,
2 cups flour	cinnamon, and nutmeg

CREAM butter, add sugar, then the milk, into which has been stirred the soda, next the spices, flour and egg, well beaten.

Mrs. Tucker.

SOUTHERN BEATEN BISCUIT

1 quart of flour	1 cup of rich milk
Piece of lard the size of an egg	1-4 teaspoonful of soda
1 heaping teaspoonful of salt	

CHOP the lard into the flour till thoroughly mixed through it, and add the other ingredients to make a stiff dough. Work this or beat it on a marble slab twenty minutes, or until it blisters. Roll it one-fourth of an inch thick, and cut or make by hand into tiny biscuit. Stick them with a fork, and bake in a quick oven for thirty minutes.

Mrs. Cowan.

BUTTERED ROLL

A PINT of flour, one heaping teaspoonful baking powder, a pinch of salt, and sweet milk enough to make a moderately stiff dough. Knead a little, roll out half an inch thick, and spread with a piece of butter the size of an egg. Sprinkle well with flour, roll up, and cut in slices an inch thick. Bake in a quick oven.

A. L. W.

EGG BISCUIT

3 pints of flour	1 cup of milk
2 eggs, the whites	Pinch of salt
1-2 cup of yeast	

MIX at eleven A. M.; roll out at four P. M. Use two sizes of cutter, putting the smaller round of dough on top, then let it rise until supper-time. Bake twenty minutes.

Mrs. Geo. H. Robbins.

ASK YOUR GROCER FOR

⇒• REX •⇐

Liquid Stove Polish

IT BLACKS RED COVERS,
IS ABSOLUTELY FIREPROOF,
AND FREE FROM SMELL.

REX LIQUID STOVE POLISH Co.
WHITMAN, MASS.

PORTLAND
✫ Star ✫
MATCHES.
WARRANTED THE
Safest, Surest, and Best
FOR HOME USE OR EXPORT.

MANUFACTURED ONLY BY

PORTLAND STAR MATCH CO.
PORTLAND, MAINE.

13

THE
F. SCHUMACHER MILLING Co.
AKRON, OHIO,

Manufacturers of

PARCHED FARINOSE and ROLLED WHEAT; .· .· .·
ROLLED AVENA, *the best product made from White Oats, put
up in Barrels, and Cases of 36 Packages, 2 lbs. each;* OATMEAL;
CRACKED WHEAT; WHOLE WINTER WHEAT
and W. W. GRAHAM FLOUR, *Always Pure, Always Reliable;*
GRANULATED, *and* COARSE PEARL HOMINY; WHITE
and YELLOW GRANULATED CORNMEAL. .· .· .· .· .·

They have recently added to their long list **a new Cereal of inestimable
value** to those suffering from impaired digestion. RICH IN GLUTEN,
GERM, GUM or DEXTRINE, it
is favorably received everywhere, **PARCHED FARINOSE.**
under the name and trade-mark of
For INFANTS, it may well supersede all other foods (save milk, which can
never find a perfect substitute during the first weeks of life), because its ready
and perfect digestion involves no strain upon feeble digestive power; it contains
all the elements demanded by the growing life. And for like reasons it is equally
adapted for INVALIDS. By FEVER PATIENTS it is used as a thin gruel,
and is partaken of with some relish even when genuine appetite and all craving
for food are suspended.
For REFINED, PROGRESSIVE HUMAN BEINGS, it will prove a
perfect food, supplying all waste, and restoring every exhausted energy.
Added to all its excellencies, its appetizing flavor will commend it to the
palates of man, woman, and child alike.
To get the genuine, call for all these goods in original packages.

14

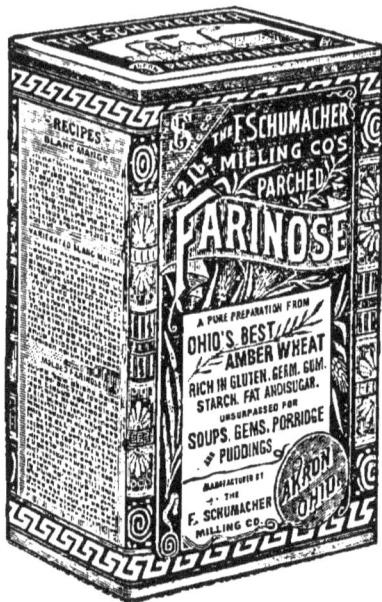

BREAKFAST CAKES, FRITTERS, AND DOUGHNUTS

''And now to breakfast with what appetite you have.''

A DELICIOUS BREAKFAST DISH

POUR two cups of boiling water on one cup of Nudavene Flakes, add a scant teaspoonful of salt, and boil one hour in a double kettle. Serve with cream.

RYE MUSH

1 quart water	1 1-2 teaspoonfuls salt
3 cups rye meal	

WHEN the water is boiling hard — not before — salt it and stir in the rye meal, putting it in gradually, stirring constantly. Let it boil briskly for five minutes, stirring occasionally to prevent sticking. Then set it on the back of the range and let it cook slowly twenty minutes more. Serve hot with sugar and cream, or milk. Many will prefer it without sugar.

Mrs. R. M. Manly.

BREAKFAST CAKES

1 1-2 cups Arlington wheat meal	1 large teaspoonful baking powder
1 egg	1 tablespoonful of sugar

MIX with milk to a thin batter, add salt, and bake in muffin or gem pans.

H. B.

WHOLE WHEAT GEMS

1 egg	1 dessertspoonful sugar
1 small tablespoonful melted butter	A little salt
1 1-3 coffee cups of milk	1 teaspoonful baking powder

MIXED with enough sifted whole wheat flour to make a batter the consistency of batter for fritters. Bake in hot gem pans in hot oven.

Mrs. Clements.

BREAKFAST GEMS

1 cup sour milk	1-2 cup of white flour sifted with 1 even teaspoonful of soda
1 teaspoonful salt	
1 cup of rye or graham flour	
	1-4 cup molasses

BEFORE beginning to make the gems, place the gem pans in the oven to get very hot; then mix the milk, molasses, and salt together. Add the flour, stir the whole thoroughly, and bake one-half hour.

Winifred E. Badger.

GRAHAM GEMS

2 cups Graham	1 piece of butter size of an egg, melted
1 cup flour	
1 egg	2 teaspoonfuls baking powder, and salt
1 pint of milk	
1 tablespoonful of sugar	

BEAT well together one-half hour before baking; heat the gem pans hot, butter well, bake in a quick oven. These cakes are very good baked as soon as mixed, but improved by standing a short time.

Mrs. T. W. Willard.

GRAHAM MUFFINS

2 cups Graham	1 teaspoonful saleratus
1 cup flour	2 teaspoonfuls cream tartar
2 tablespoonfuls molasses or 1 tablespoonful sugar	Salt

MIX with milk, or use one egg and mix with water.

Mrs. Lewis M. Grant.

RYE BREAKFAST CAKES

2 cups of rye meal
1-2 cup molasses
A little salt

1 1-2 cups of sweet milk to
mix it very soft
1 teaspoonful of saleratus

BAKE at once in a roll pan or muffin rings.

Mrs. Caswell.

RYE MUFFINS

2 cups sour milk
3 cups rye meal
1 cup flour
1 small cup molasses

2 eggs
1 teaspoonful soda
A little salt.

Mrs. Stoddard.

RYE GEMS

1 cup rye meal
1 cup Arlington flour
1 teaspoonful Royal Baking
Powder

2 large spoonfuls of sugar
1 saltspoonful of salt
1 egg thoroughly beaten
1 cup of milk

MIX in the order given, sift meal and flour *twice* and sift in the baking powder. Heat the gem pan hot and well buttered for a rich crust.

A. M. Wilson.

RYE GEMS

1 egg
1-2 cup sugar
1 cup buttermilk
1 teaspoonful soda

1 cup rye meal
2-3 cup flour
2 tablespoonfuls melted butter

MIX in the order given, and bake in hot gem pans.

Mrs. Benj. H. Sanborn.

THIN JOHNNY CAKE

2 eggs
1 1-2 cups sweet milk
Butter 1-2 size of an egg
1 tablespoonful molasses
1 cup granulated corn meal

scant teaspoonful soda
scant teaspoonfuls cream
tartar or two good teaspoonfuls of baking powder
A pinch of salt

BEAT the eggs light; add milk, salt, molasses, melted butter; sift the soda and cream of tartar with the meal, and stir it in last. Bake about a half an hour in a hot oven, in a *thin* sheet.

Mrs. R. M. Manly.

CORN MEAL BREAKFAST CAKES

Scald 1 cup of corn meal
Add sufficient milk to make quite thin
Pinch of salt

1-2 cup flour
Heaping teaspoonful baking powder

BAKE on a griddle.

Mrs. Caswell.

BREAKFAST CORN CAKE

1 cupful corn meal
1 cupful flour
1 teaspoonful Royal Baking Powder

2 large spoonfuls of sugar
1 saltspoonful of salt
1 egg well beaten
Milk enough for a thick batter

SIFT the meal and flour twice, and sift in the baking powder; mix in the order given. Melt a tablespoonful of butter in the spider; pour about half of it into the mixture, and bake the cake in the spider, the melted butter forming a rich crust; will bake in twenty minutes in a hot oven.

Anna M. Wilson.

CORN CAKE

1 egg
1-2 cup sugar
1-2 cup flour
2 teaspoonfuls baking powder

Salt
1 tablespoonful butter
1 cup milk
1 1-2 cups Indian meal.

Mrs. A. Jennings.

OENDORFF

2 cups of hominy, after it is boiled
1 cup of milk

1 tablespoonful of butter
2 eggs

BAKE in deep pie plates about twenty minutes to half an hour. Good breakfast dish.

Mrs. C. P. Withington.

RAISED MUFFINS

1 pint milk
Piece of butter the size of an egg

1 saltspoonful salt
1-2 cup yeast

FLOUR for batter rather thicker than for griddle cakes. Mix in the morning, if for tea. When the batter is light, having been kept in a warm place, fill the rings half full, and let the muffins rise until the rings are full. Bake in a quick oven. Let them rise from one to two hours.

Mrs. Edwin B. Webb.

RAISED MUFFINS

1-3 cup sugar	1 egg
1-4 cup butter	Flour enough to make a
1-2 pint milk	stiff batter
1-4 cake yeast	

DISSOLVE the yeast cake in a little *warm* water, thicken it with flour, and let it rise half an hour. Cream the butter and sugar, warm the milk, and mix; let it rise over night. Stir it down in the morning. Add the egg well beaten; put into small tins when well risen, bake half an hour.

Mrs. Benj. H. Sanborn.

COFFEE ROLLS

12 cups flour	1 yeast cake
1 cup white sugar	3 eggs
1-2 cup butter or lard	3 large cups warm milk

LET rise over night. If well risen in the morning, knead and set in cool place till 3 P. M. Shape in long rolls, and let rise an hour and a half. Bake half an hour in a moderate oven.

C. E. Cameron.

MUFFINS

1 pint milk	1-4 cup sugar
2 eggs	

BEAT the eggs and sugar together and add the milk. Stir into this one quart of flour, three teaspoonfuls yeast powder, salt, and a small piece of lard, melted.

Mrs. N. H. Dadmun.

MUFFINS

THREE cups of flour, two teaspoonfuls of cream of tartar, one teaspoonful of soda. Mix with it one egg, one tablespoonful of sugar, three of melted butter, a little salt, and two cups of sweet milk. Bake in gem pans.

Mrs. J. Moulton.

CREAM TARTAR MUFFINS

1 quart flour	1 teaspoonful saleratus
1 small pint rich milk	2 teaspoonfuls cream tartar
2 eggs	Salt
1 tablespoonful sugar	

MIX salt, sugar, cream tartar, dry in flour, add eggs without beating, then milk with saleratus dissolved in it, and beat thoroughly. Bake in gem pans in quick oven.

Mrs. C. E. Shattuck.

MUFFINS

1 quart flour	2 teaspoonfuls cream tartar
2 cups milk	1 teaspoonful soda
1-2 cup sugar	A little salt
2 eggs	Butter the size of an egg

MELT the butter with four tablespoonfuls of boiling water. Beat thoroughly. Bake in muffin pans thirty minutes in a quick oven.

Mrs. Mary L. Whipple.

LEBANON MUFFINS

2 eggs	1 pint flour
1 teacup cream, or sweet milk	1 teaspoonful baking pow-
Butter 1-2 size of an egg	der

BEAT the yolks, and add milk and melted butter. Mix the baking powder with the flour and add to the above, and stir in the beaten whites last. Will make one dozen in gem or muffin pan.

Miss Kendall.

· POPOVERS

1 pint sweet milk, 1 pint flour, 1 egg

BAKE in iron gem pans.

Mrs. Tucker.

BLUEBERRY CAKE

1 pint flour	2 teaspoonfuls cream tartar
1 teaspoonful soda	2 eggs
1-2 pint milk	

Mrs. Edwin B. Webb.

BERRY CAKE

Butter size of an egg	1 egg
1-2 cup sugar	1-2 teaspoonful saleratus
1 cup milk	1 teaspoonful cream tartar
1 teaspoonful salt	2 cups flour (before sifted)
1 cup berries	

Miss Hall.

BLUEBERRY CAKE

2 eggs	1 teaspoonful cream tartar
1 cup sugar	1-2 teaspoonful soda
1 cup milk	Pint berries
2 cups flour	

Miss Mary Mason.

BLUEBERRY CAKE

4 cupfuls flour	1 1-2 teaspoonfuls cream of tartar
1 cupful milk	1 teaspoonful soda
1 cupful sugar	1 pint berries, rubbed in a dish of flour
2 eggs	
1-2 cupful melted butter	

Mrs. Mary L. Whipple.

ORANGE SHORTCAKE

1 egg	2-3 cup of sweet milk
1-2 cup of sugar	1 1-4 cups of flour
2 tablespoonfuls of melted butter	1 teaspoonful Royal Baking · Powder

BAKE in a round pan. Split while hot. Fill with oranges that have been previously sliced, well sugared, and the seeds removed.

Ellen Morris.

HEALTHFUL SHORTCAKE

1 pint rich, fresh buttermilk   1 quart nice ripe strawberries
1 teaspoonful baking soda   A little salt
Graham flour

To the milk add soda, salt, and sufficient Graham flour to make a tolerably stiff batter. Bake this in two pans (as for jelly cake) in a brisk oven. Have ready the strawberries, or any kind of fruit desired, mashed and sweetened to taste.

When the cakes are baked, split and butter them, spread upon the halves the prepared fruit and put them together again.

This may be eaten either hot or cold, and with cream.

Elizabeth R. Horr.

FOOL'S WONDERS

ONE and one-half cups of sour milk, one egg, flour enough to roll thin about the size of a tea plate, a little salt, one-half teaspoonful of soda. Fry as doughnuts. Apples stewed and sweetened and spread between each layer.

C. S. Flagg.

WAFFLES

1 quart of flour   2 teaspoonfuls of cream of
4 eggs   tartar
2 tablespoonfuls of butter   1 teaspoonful of soda
                         A little salt

MAKE a batter with milk, and bake in very hot waffle irons.

Mrs. Pomeroy.

WAFFLES

2 eggs   1 teaspoonful Royal Baking
1 cup milk   Powder
1 pint flour   1-2 teaspoonful salt
                   1 tablespoonful butter, melted

PUT a spoonful in each compartment of waffle iron, close the cover and cook one minute on one side, turn and cook a little longer on the other. Serve with syrup.

Ellen Morris.

RAISED DOUGHNUTS

1 egg
1 cup sugar
1-2 cup butter

1-2 yeast cake
1 pint milk (scalded)
Little salt and nutmeg

MIX butter and sugar, then add the beaten egg, then the scalded milk and yeast, mix as stiff as bread, let rise over night. In the morning roll out about a quarter of an inch thick, cut in squares about three inches, let them stand an hour before raising.

Mrs. J. E. Selfe.

DOUGHNUTS

1 cup sugar
1 cup milk
2 eggs
Piece of butter size of an egg
1 teaspoonful soda

2 cream tartar
Spice
Wheat Meal sufficient to roll
out

A. W. M.

DOUGHNUTS

2 cupfuls sugar
2 eggs
1 cupful milk
2 tablespoonfuls butter

1 heaping teaspoonful baking
powder
A little salt

BEAT the sugar and eggs together. Mix soft. Have the lard very hot.

Mrs. Mary L. Whipple.

DOUGHNUTS

2 eggs
1 1-2 cups sugar
1 1-2 cups sour milk
2 tablespoonfuls butter

1-2 teaspoonful saleratus, salt
and nutmeg
Flour

E. O. K.

DOUGHNUTS

1 cup sugar
1 egg
1 large spoonful melted butter
1 cup buttermilk

1 teaspoonful soda
A little salt and nutmeg
Flour to make a rather soft
dough

CUT into rings with an open cutter. Fry in hot fat.

Ellen Morris.

RYE PAN CAKES

2 eggs	1 tablespoonful molasses
1 cup sugar	1-2 cup flour
2 cups milk (sweet or sour)	Nutmeg and rose water

THICKEN with rye meal so that the dough will pour easily from a spoon. If sour milk is used, add a rising teaspoonful of soda. If sweet milk, one of soda and two of cream tartar.

E. Marietta Dewing.

COCOA

1 pint hot water	1 teacup brown sugar
1 pint sweet milk	1 egg beaten thoroughly with
4 teaspoonfuls cocoa, or	1-2 cup very hot, though not
2 squares grated chocolate	boiling water
2 teaspoonfuls of corn starch dissolved in 1-2 cup milk	

POUR the water over the cocoa in a granite pot, then add the milk and sugar, beating thoroughly. When this boils up add the dissolved corn starch very slowly. Let all boil together well for some five or ten minutes, when the cocoa is ready. Break the egg into a quart bowl and pour over it one-half cup very hot water, and beat it with a Dover egg beater till the bowl is nearly full of the froth. Pour some of this into the cocoa pot, then pour in the boiling cocoa, reserving some of the egg for the top, and serve. This makes eight cups of delightful cocoa.

Mrs. Cowan.

APPLE FRITTERS

YOLKS of two eggs beaten well; add half a cup of milk or water, and one tablespoonful of olive oil, one teaspoonful of sugar, one saltspoonful of salt, and one cup of flour, or enough to make it almost a drop batter. When ready to use, add the whites of the eggs, beaten very stiff. Core and pare three or four apples, but do not break them. Cut them in slices one-third of an inch thick, leaving the opening in the centre. Dip each slice in the fritter batter and fry in hot fat. Drain and sprinkle with powdered sugar, lemon, and spice. If bananas are used, cut lengthwise and treat in same manner.

Mrs. Albert Jennings.

BANANA FRITTERS

3 eggs	2 teaspoonfuls baking powder
1 pint milk	1-2 teaspoonful salt
2 teacups flour	2 bananas

BEAT the eggs thoroughly, add milk, and stir in flour, with which the powder has been well mixed while dry. Slice in the bananas, and drop by spoonful into hot lard.

Mrs. Peabody.

APPLE FRITTERS

1 teacupful milk	2 teaspoonfuls baking powder
1 beaten egg	A pinch of salt

THICKEN with flour enough to prevent the batter from sticking to the spoon. Slice two or three sour apples very thin and mix them with the batter. Drop into hot lard, and fry like doughnuts. Eat with syrup, or cream and sugar.

Mrs. Wilson.

OATMEAL GRIDDLE CAKES

1 pint cold boiled oatmeal	2 teaspoonfuls Royal Baking
1 cup milk	Powder
1-2 teaspoonful salt	2 eggs
2 cups flour	

BEAT the milk into the oatmeal, add the salt, the yolks of the eggs, and a cup of boiling water, mixing all well together. Add the flour and beat again; add the baking powder and continue beating. Beat the whites of the eggs to a stiff froth and add to the mixture, and mix well together. Bake on a hot buttered griddle.

FLOUR GRIDDLE CAKES

1 pint sour milk	2 eggs
A little butter	1 heaping teaspoonful soda
Salt	Flour for a soft batter

Mrs. Stoddard.

FRENCH TOAST

BEAT two eggs and stir them into a pint of milk. Slice home-made bread ; dip the pieces into the eggs and milk, fry brown in hot butter.   Sprinkle sugar on each piece and serve hot.

Mrs. Wilson.

PHYSICIANS' PRESCRIPTIONS

ACCURATELY and HONESTLY
COMPOUNDED.

CHARLES W. PERRY,
Apothecary,
No. 9 WEST CENTRAL STREET, NATICK.

FOR FLAVORING, USE
Perry's Star Flavoring Extracts.
THEIR PURITY GUARANTEED.

The Best Laundry Starch
in the World.

ELECTRIC LUSTRE STARCH

*Makes Collars and Cuffs
look like new.
Will not stick to the Iron.
Saves Time, Trouble,
and Labor.*

Electric Lustre Starch
*is also highly prized by
ladies as a* **TOILET
POWDER.**
As a **FLESH POWDER
FOR INFANTS** *it is
unequalled.*

For sale by all grocers

27

DOBBINS' ● ● ● ● ● ● ●

∴ Electric Soap

Is for sale everywhere, and has for twenty years
been acknowledged by all to be the

BEST FAMILY SOAP in the WORLD.

In order to bring its merits to the notice of a still larger constituency, we have
recently reduced our price, keeping its quality unchanged, and offer the following

BEAUTIFUL PRESENTS

free of all expense, to all who will preserve, and mail to us, with their full address,

The Pictures of Mrs. Fogy cut from the Outside Wrappers taken from this Soap.

For Fifteen Pictures we will mail a beautiful book, 56 pages,

SHORT HINTS ON SOCIAL ETIQUETTE,

the cash price of which is forty cents; or a new and beautiful set of seven
Cabinet Portraits of

D'OYLEY CARTE'S ORIGINAL ENGLISH MIKADO COMPANY, Fifth Avenue Theatre, New York City.

For Twenty-five Pictures we will mail the most beautiful Panel Picture
ever published   We have several superb subjects, and in ordering please
specify either

"LES INTIMES," "THE TWO SISTERS," or "L'HIVER."

The original paintings are owned by us, and cannot be copied or duplicated
by any other firm, and hence the Panels are worthy a place in any house in
the land. For twenty-five Pictures we will mail, free of postage, the following six (6) unabridged popular novels:

A Dangerous Woman, by Mrs. A. S. STEPHENS.
From the Earth to the Moon, by JULES VERNE.
The Story of a Wedding Ring, by the author of "Dora Thorne."
The Peril of Richard Pardon, by FARJEON.
Clouds and Sunshine, by CHARLES READE.
Ruthven's Ward, by FLORENCE MARRYAT.
Only one lot of these novels will be sent to one address.

The housekeeper will find on a trial, *according to directions*, that the washing
does not require HALF THE QUANTITY OF DOBBINS' ELECTRIC
SOAP that it does of *any other;* that there is a great saving of time and labor in
its use; that it saves the wear and tear of the clothes on the washboard, and does
not cut or rot them to pieces, or hurt the hands, as adulterated soaps do.

IT DISINFECTS CLOTHES WASHED WITH IT,

leaving them thoroughly cleansed and sweet, instead of adding a foul odor of
rosin and filthy grease. ☞ It washes flannels *without shrinking*, leaving them
soft and nice.

I. L. CRAGIN & CO.,

Manufacturers Dobbins' Electric Soap,

No. 119 S. 4th St., PHILADELPHIA, PA.

28

SOUP

"Every cook praises her own stew."

POTATO SOUP

1 quart milk	1 onion
6 large potatoes	1 tablespoonful butter
1 stalk celery	

PUT the milk to boil with onion and celery. Pare potatoes, and boil thirty minutes. Turn off the water, and mash fine and light. Add the boiling milk and the butter, and pepper and salt to taste. Rub through a strainer and serve immediately. A cup of whipped cream is an improvement.

Mrs. Edwin B. Webb.

CREAM SOUP

1 tablespoonful flour	Salt as needed
1 tablespoonful butter	Celery extract, or onion, cat-
1 quart boiling water	sup, lemon, sage leaf, or any
1 egg	other flavoring preferred

RUB the flour smooth in the butter, stir into the boiling water and bring to a quick boil. Set off from the fire for two or three minutes, stir in the egg beaten, then cover immediately in a *hot* tureen.

Mary E. Horton.

CLAM SOUP

STRAIN one quart clams and chop fine. Put piece of butter large as an egg into the kettle (or fry out several pieces of salt pork), then put in clams and the liquor. Add one quart cold water, two onions cut very fine, salt, pepper, and one teaspoonful sugar. Boil very slowly, tightly covered, for two hours, then stir in pint milk, and at the last one tablespoonful flour mixed smoothly.

.Mrs. Watson.

MOCK BISQUE SOUP

Stew a can of tomatoes and strain, add a pinch of soda to remove acidity; in another saucepan boil three pints of milk thickened with a tablespoonful of corn starch, previously mixed with a little cold milk; add a lump of butter size of an egg, salt and pepper to taste; mix with tomatoes; let all come to a boil and serve.

Mrs. Benj. H. Sanborn.

TOMATO SOUP

1 quart of canned tomatoes	1 pint milk
3 teaspoonfuls of sugar	1-2 tablepoonful flour
1 teaspoonful salt	

After boiling the tomatoes fifteen minutes, strain them and add water sufficient to increase the quantity, then stir in the sugar and salt.

Put the milk into a vessel and set into hot water, stir in the flour slowly until the milk is thickened, then add this to the tomato, and let the whole boil five minutes.

Winifred E. Badger.

SPLIT PEA SOUP

1-2 pint split peas	1 tablespoonful flour
2 quarts cold water	1 teaspoonful sugar
2 tablespoonfuls butter	1 1-2 cups milk

Soak the peas *over night* in cold water. Drain and put them on to boil in two quarts of cold water. When soft rub through a *colander*, then through a *sieve*, and put on to boil again. Add the milk, thicken with the flour rubbed smooth in the butter; season with salt and white pepper.

BOUILLON

5 lbs. juicy beef	4 pepper corns
2 quarts cold water	1 small onion with 4 cloves

SIMMER six hours, strain and cool, skim, heat and season to taste.

A. M. C.

GREEN CORN SOUP

7 large ears of corn	1 tablespoonful butter
1 quart water	1 teaspoonful flour
1 pint milk	1 teaspoonful sugar

CUT through each row of kernels with a sharp knife. With the back of the knife, scrape out the pulp. Boil the cobs thirty minutes in one quart of water; strain, add the pulp, and boil ten minutes. Add the milk and sugar, thicken with the butter and flour cooked together. Boil up once, season with salt and white pepper, and serve. Corn a little hard is better for soup.

Mrs. Benj. H. Sanborn.

TOMATO SOUP WITH MILK

BOIL one quart milk, thicken with one tablespoonful of flour, one tablespoonful of butter, little pepper and salt, then one pint strained tomato with a pinch of soda added. Serve at once.

Mrs. Stoddard.

Adams Express

∴ Company ∴

forwards to all parts of the United States.

Special attention paid to business between

Wellesley and Boston. 7 Expresses each way Daily. Rates as low as by any responsible company.

Office, Wellesley, at Karbs' Shoe Store. F. N. BASSETT, Agt.

Parents, Attention!

• • • • • • *E*XAMINE *the*

Monitor School Shoe

for Misses and Children, both tipped and plain toe. Warranted to give satisfaction.

Also, FOOT WEAR of ALL DESCRIPTIONS.

AL. W. KARBS.

ASK YOUR SHOE DEALER FOR

GILT EDGE

THE LADIES' FAVORITE.

ONCE TRIED, ALWAYS USED.

BOTTLES HOLD DOUBLE QUANTITY.   PRICE, 25c.

WHITTEMORE BROS. & CO.,

Sole Manufacturers,

BOSTON, MASS.

33

An Unbroken Record *DURYEA'S Glen Cove Manu-facturing Co. received the ONLY* of Success. *GOLD MEDAL, over all competitors, at PARIS EXPOSITION, 1889.*

Duryea's
Satin Gloss Starch

Gives a Beautiful, White, Glossy, and Lasting Finish.

NO OTHER STARCH SO EASILY USED OR SO ECONOMICAL.

Duryea's
Improved Corn Starch.

From the *BEST SELECTED INDIAN CORN*, and *WARRANTED PERFECTLY PURE.*

DURYEA'S STARCH,

In every instance of competition, has received the highest award.

In addition to Medals, many Diplomas have been received. The following are a few of the characterizing terms of award:

At London, 1862, for quality	"EXCEEDINGLY EXCELLENT."
Paris, 1867, " "	"PERFECTION OF PREPARATION."
Paris, 1878, " "	"BEST PRODUCTION OF ITS KIND."
Centennial, 1876, for	"NOTABLE OR ABSOLUTE PURITY."
Brussels, 1876, for	"REMARKABLE EXCELLENCE."
Franklin Institute, Penn.,	"FOR SUPERIOR MERIT, not alone as being

THE BEST OF THE KIND EXHIBITED, but as
THE BEST KNOWN TO EXIST IN THE MARKET OF AMERICAN PRODUCTION."

FOR SALE BY GROCERS GENERALLY.

34

FISH

" Old Ocean's treasures."

TO BROIL FISH

CLEAN, wash, and wipe dry. Split, so that when laid flat, the backbone will be in the middle. Sprinkle with salt, and lay, inside down, upon a buttered gridiron over a clear fire until it is nicely colored, then turn. When done, put upon a hot dish, butter plentifully, and pepper. Put a hot cover over it and send to table.

BAKED FISH

A FISH weighing from four to six pounds is a good size to bake. It should be cooked whole to look well. Make dressing of bread crumbs, butter, salt, and a little salt pork chopped fine (parsley and onions, if you please); mix this with one egg. Fill the body, sew it up, lay in large dripper; put across it some strips of salt pork to flavor it. Put pint water and little salt in pan. Bake an hour and a half. Baste frequently. After taking up fish, thicken gravy and pour over it.

CREAM GRAVY FOR BAKED FISH. — Have ready in saucepan cup of cream, diluted with a few spoonfuls hot water; stir in carefully two tablespoonfuls melted butter and a little chopped parsley; heat this in vessel filled with hot water. Pour in gravy from dripping pan of fish.

FISH CHOWDER

1 dozen potatoes sliced coarsely	1 pint rich milk
	1 tablespoonful flour
1 small haddock sliced	6 crackers toasted
5 slices salt pork chopped	Salt and pepper
2 small onions sliced	

PLACE fish and potatoes in kettle and cover with water. Fry the pork, and skim out and place in the kettle; fry the onions in the pork fat, add the whole to the fish and potatoes; boil until the potatoes are done, then, just before removing from fire, add the flour dissolved in milk, and seasoning.

Place crackers in dish, pour over them the chowder.

A. M. C.

FISH BALLS

1 cup raw salt fish	1 egg well beaten
2 cups raw potatoes	Saltspoonful pepper
1 teaspoonful butter	.

COOK the fish and potatoes together till the potatoes are soft. Then mash well and add the butter and egg. Fry in hot fat.

Pauline Smith.

SCALLOPED CODFISH

1 lb. salt codfish	3 tablespoonfuls butter
1 cup of milk	1 cup bread crumbs
3 eggs	

BOIL the fish and chop it fine. Hard-boil the eggs, and after chopping fine add to the fish. Put a part of the bread crumbs on the bottom of a dish, then a little of the milk heated with the butter, then fish and egg, and so on, leaving enough crumbs for a thick layer on top. Cover with bits of butter, and bake thirty minutes.

New Lebanon, N. Y.

SCALLOPED FISH

ONE pound of fish boiled half an hour; put one teaspoonful salt and vinegar in the water. When done, break in small pieces and place it in the dish you are going to serve it in. Salt and pepper to taste; take one and one-half cups of milk and let come to a boil, thicken with one-quarter cup melted butter, and flour to make a paste; pour this over the fish. Half-dozen crackers rolled fine, mixed with a quarter cup butter; spread over the top, and bake twenty or thirty minutes.

Catherine S. Flagg.

BROILED SALT MACKEREL

FRESHEN by soaking it over night in water, taking care that the skin lies uppermost. In the morning dry it without breaking, cut off the head and tip of the tail, place it between the bars of a buttered fish-gridiron, and broil to a light brown, lay it on a hot dish, and dress with a little butter, pepper, and lemon juice, vinegar, or chopped pickle.

SALMON CROQUETTES

1 lb. salmon	1 egg
1 cup cream or milk	1 cup bread crumbs
2 tablespoonfuls butter	1 tablespoonful flour

MIX flour and butter together, and stir with the beaten egg into the milk when quite hot. Pour over the salmon and large cup of bread crumbs; mix well, and when cold, shape and roll in egg and bread crumbs, and fry in deep fat, or make flat cakes and fry in frypan with less fat.

New Lebanon, N. Y.

RICE CROQUETTES

2 cups cold boiled rice	3 eggs
2 tablespoonfuls melted butter	1 teaspoonful sugar

WORK the butter in the rice, then add the beaten eggs and flour enough to mould. Roll in egg and powdered cracker. Fry in deep fat.

VEAL CROQUETTES

CHOP cold veal and about one-fourth or one-third as much cold ham quite fine. Stir it into a milk sauce (milk thickened with flour and butter very thick).

While hot, season highly and let it cool. Then shape into croquettes, roll in cracker crumbs, and fry as usual.

J. TAILBY & SON,
Opp. Railroad Station,
WELLESLEY.

Florists.

CUT · FLOWERS · AND · PLANTS
of the choicest varieties, constantly on hand.

FLORAL DESIGNS for all occasions arranged at shortest notice.
Orders by mail or otherwise promptly attended to.
Flowers carefully packed, and forwarded to all parts of the **United States**
and **Canada.**

COLBURN'S

THE KING OF
CONDIMENTS.

PHILADELPHIA

THE FINEST
MUSTARD MADE.

MUSTARD.

Sold only in 1-4 lb., 1-2 lb., and 1 lb. cans.

THE A. COLBURN CO.,

MUSTARDS AND SPICES,

PHILADELPHIA, PA.

W. F. CLELAND,

Dry and Fancy Goods.

New Wash Goods just opening :
GINGHAMS, *Percales, Victoria*
Cloths, Indigos, Surahs, etc.

Large and Complete Line
HOSIERY, *Gloves, Corsets, and*
Smallwares.

Sole Agent for FOSTER, PAUL & CO.'S OWN MAKE GLOVES.

9 Clark's Block, Main Street . . . . NATICK.

39

John H. Pray, Sons & Co.

EXTRA SUPER

CARPETS.

THE choice of our entire stock of over four hundred patterns and colorings, and including all of our Lowell Extra Supers, as well as many other RELIABLE makes, at **70c.** PER YARD.

.⁕ .⁕ .⁕

Also, quite a large line of patterns that we shall not have manufactured again, but identically the same goods as the above in all other respects, at **60c.** PER YARD.

Roxbury Tapestries.

WE SHOW, without exception, the entire line of patterns produced by the ROXBURY CARPET CO., and offer any Roxbury Carpet in our whole stock at · · · · · · · **85c.** PER YARD.

.⁕ .⁕ .⁕

In both EXTRA SUPERS and TAPESTRIES we have many private patterns that are our own exclusive property, and cannot be found elsewhere.

John H. Pray, Sons & Co.

CARPETS and UPHOLSTERY,

558 and 560 Washington Street,
30 to 34 Harrison Avenue Extension.

OYSTERS

'' The man who first an Oyster ate, we read,
Had made his will before the reckless deed.''

BISQUE OF OYSTERS

PUT two quarts of oysters in a saucepan with white pepper, two ounces of butter, nutmeg, two blades of mace, a bay leaf, a pinch of red pepper, and a pint of white broth. Cover and boil ten minutes. Drain in a colander and save the liquor.

Chop the oysters very fine, and put on a plate. Knead five ounces of flour in a saucepan with four ounces of melted butter. Stir and cook a little, without allowing it to brown. Dilute with three pints of boiled milk and the oyster liquor.

Add oysters, stir steadily, and boil ten minutes and rub thoroughly through a very fine sieve. Add more milk, if required, stir, and boil again.

Finish with half a pint of raw cream and four ounces of butter in small bits. Taste, pour into a tureen and serve with small squares of bread fried in butter, and served separately.

M. H. L.

SCALLOPED OYSTERS

1 quart oysters	1-2 cup butter
1 lb. milk crackers	Salt and pepper
1 quart rich milk	

ROLL the crackers and place a layer on bottom of dish, place next a layer of oysters, with bits of butter, salt and pepper; fill the dish with alternate layers of cracker and oysters, having cracker on the top. Pour over them the milk and oyster broth; cover and bake briskly one hour, uncover and brown.

This may be varied by adding a well-beaten egg and a trifle of nutmeg.

Serve with slices of lemon.

A. M. C.

OYSTERS EN COQUILLE

FILL oyster or scallop shells with oysters; season with salt, butter, pepper, and lemon juice, cover with sifted buttered bread crumbs. Bake till the crumbs are brown. Place the shells on small plates and serve.

M. T.

CREAMED OYSTERS

1 pint oysters	1 tablespoonful of flour
1 pint cream (rich milk is very good)	Small piece of onion and of mace

LET the cream with mace and onion come to a boil, mix the flour with a little cold milk and stir it into the cream. Let the oysters come to a boil in their own liquor, skim carefully, drain off all the liquor, turn the oysters into the cream, skim out the mace and onion, and serve.

Mrs. T. W. Willard.

OYSTER CAKES FOR BREAKFAST

ONE pint oysters chopped into very small pieces and seasoned with pepper and salt. Add the liquor, one beaten egg, and rolled cracker enough to hold stiff so it can be fried, a spoonful at a time, on a hot griddle — *browning both sides,* and making very small cakes.

FRIED OYSTERS

SELECT largest and finest oysters. Drain and wipe them by spreading upon cloth, laying another over them, pressing lightly. Roll each in beaten egg, then in cracker crumbs with which has been mixed a very little pepper. Fry in mixture of equal parts of lard and butter.

R. B. P.

OYSTER SHORTCAKE

2 1-2 cups flour	3 teaspoonfuls baking powder
1 cup sweet milk	Salt
1 egg	

BAKE as shortcake, split and fill with creamed oysters, viz., —

| 1 quart oysters | 1-2 cup butter |
| 1 cup cream | 1 tablespoonful of corn starch |

M. H. L.

OYSTER PIE

ONE quart oysters drained; pepper, salt, and butter to taste. One quart of flour, two tablespoonfuls of lard, one teaspoonful baking powder, one-half teaspoonful salt. Mix with water for crust. Butter and line pie-plate with the crust; fill with the oyster, seasoned; cover with crust and bake.

R. B. P.

CLAM FRITTERS

1 quart clams	2 eggs
1 pint flour	Salt and pepper
1-2 pint milk	

MAKE a batter of flour, eggs, and milk, and stir in clams. Drop in spoonfuls into hot fat, and fry brown on both sides.

A. M. C.

EGGS

" The turnpike road to people's hearts, I find,
Lies through their mouths, or I mistake mankind."

CREAMED EGGS

BOIL six eggs twenty minutes. Make one pint of cream sauce. Have six slices of toast in a hot dish; put a layer of sauce on each one, and then a part of the whites of the eggs, cut into thin strips. Rub a part of the yolks through a sieve upon the toast. Repeat this and finish with a third layer of sauce. Place in the oven for about three minutes. Garnish with parsley, and serve hot.

Mrs. Edwin B. Webb.

EGG BASKETS

BOIL eggs twenty minutes, shell, cut in halves, take out the yolks, and take slices from the points of each half white, *that the baskets may stand.* Put the yolks in a dish and mash fine, add equal quantity of finely chopped ham, chicken, or tongue; season with salt, pepper, and mustard. Add and mix melted butter, and *shape into round balls* size of the yolk, putting one into each basket. Set these on rounds of buttered toast a little larger than the baskets.

A white sauce, as for cream toast, may be poured around, and sprigs of parsley placed on top of each ball make a pretty garnish.

SCALLOPED EGGS

6 eggs	1-4 cup melted butter
1 pint white sauce	1 cup ham, veal, tongue, or
1 cup cracker crumbs	poultry

BOIL eggs twenty minutes, moisten the cracker crumbs with the melted butter, chop fine the meat, remove the yolks of the eggs, and chop whites fine.

Put a layer of buttered crumbs in a buttered scallop dish, then a layer of chopped whites, white sauce, meat, yolks rubbed through a strainer, and so on, till all the material is used, having buttered crumbs on the top. Bake till crumbs are brown.

Mrs. Spear.

BAKED EGGS

BREAK each one in a cup, being careful not to break the yolk. Lay the eggs one by one in a hot buttered dish, put a little salt on each egg, and bake till firm ; add a little butter and serve at once.

A Nicer Way

COVER a buttered dish with fine cracker crumbs. Put each egg carefully into dish and cover it *lightly* with cracker, butter, and seasoning, and *bake until the crumbs brown.*

BEST WAY OF BOILING EGGS

PUT the eggs into a saucepan and cover with boiling water and let stand where the water will keep hot, *yet not boil,* for ten minutes.

If eggs are to be *hard*-boiled, cook them in this way twenty minutes. The yolk will be dry and mealy, and easily rubbed smooth.

APPLE OMELETTE

1 pint strained apple sauce
3 eggs beaten separately

1 teacup sugar
2 tablespoonfuls melted butter

BEAT apples, sugar, butter, and yellows well together. Lastly add the whites, beaten as for cake. Bake in a greased pudding dish. Serve cold with or without cream.

Mrs. Cowan.

PLAIN OMELETTE

3 eggs   3 tablespoonfuls milk

BEAT whites and yolks of eggs separately, turn into bowl and add milk. Stir lightly together.

Have a spider hot and pour mixture into it. As soon as it is a delicate brown on the bottom and is just set or cooked, but not *stiff,* put into the oven just to dry off top — a very short time is sufficient. Have a platter hot, and then fold together the omelette and turn on to it.

Serve immediately. The omelette must be cooked as soon as prepared. Standing spoils it.

Mrs. C. E. Shattuck.

OMELETTE

2 eggs
1 tablespoonful corn starch (small)
1-2 cup of milk

Lump of butter size of horsechestnut
Salt

BEAT the yolks, flour, and milk together, add the butter melted; beat the whites of the eggs to a stiff froth and add them the last thing.

Grease a spider thoroughly with butter, and when hot put in the omelette and cook on top of stove.

It takes about five minutes and needs very careful watching; when done turn one half over on to the other and serve at once.

Mrs. Pomeroy.

BAKED OMELETTE

1 pint milk   4 eggs   1 tablespoonful flour

SCALD the milk and thicken with the flour; let it cool a little, then add the eggs, yolks and whites beaten separately, and a little salt. Pour into a buttered dish, and bake until it rises all over like a custard.

Mrs. C. P. Withington.

SIASCONSETT OMELETTE

5 eggs   Butter size of half an egg
2-3 cup of milk   Salt and pepper

SEPARATE three whites, beat the five yolks and two whites; add the milk, pepper, and salt, to taste. Put the butter into the frying-pan, heat and pour in the above mixture. If air bubbles rise, prick them. Have ready the three whites beaten stiff, and when the above is cooked through spread over the whites, with a sprinkle of salt, and place in the oven till the whites are a *little* stiffened. Loosen with a knife and roll out on a warm platter.

OMELETTE

1 1-2 cups hot, not boiled, milk   1 tablespoonful of flour
5 eggs, yolks and whites   1 tablespoonful of butter
   beaten separately   1 teaspoonful of salt

BAKE twenty minutes in a hot oven and serve at once. Do not move it after once put into the oven till it is taken out.

A. M. Wilson.

MEAT

"Live not to eat, but eat to live."

ROAST BEEF

SEVEN pounds of sirloin ór the back of the rump. Wash, trim, tie or skewer into shape, and lay on a rack in the pan, and dredge all over with salt and flour. Put into a very hot oven at first, to sear the meat and keep in the juices. Put pieces of the fat beef into the pan. When well seared, baste (with the fat) and turn often, and reduce the heat. Bake one hour, if liked *rare*, an hour and a half well done. Add a little hot water to the pan if there is danger of the fat burning.

YORKSHIRE PUDDING

Serve as a Garnish to Roast Beef.

BEAT three eggs very light; add one scant pint of milk and one-half teaspoonful of salt. Pour this mixture slowly over two-thirds of a cup of flour, beating all the time until smooth. Bake in hot gem pans three-quarters of an hour. Baste twice with drippings from the beef.

GRAVY FOR ROAST BEEF

WHEN the meat is done, if more than a half-cup of fat, pour it out and mix two heaping tablespoonfuls of flour *smooth* with the fat in the pan and pour one and one-half pints of boiling water on, a little at a time; boil a little, strain, and serve.

Mrs. Benj. H. Sanborn.

SCOTCH ROLL

5 lbs. flank of beef	1-8 teaspoonful clove
3 tablespoonfuls salt	1 teaspoonful summer savory
1 tablespoonful sugar	3 tablespoonfuls vinegar
1-2 teaspoonful pepper	

REMOVE the tough skin from the beef. A portion of meat will be found thicker than the rest. With a sharp knife cut a thin layer from the thick part and lay upon the thin. Mix together the salt, sugar, pepper, clove, and summer savory* and sprinkle over the meat, and then sprinkle with the vinegar. Roll up and tie. Put away in a cold place for twelve hours; then put in stewpan and cover with boiling water. Simmer gently for three and one-half hours. Mix four tablespoonfuls of flour with half a cup of cold water and stir into the gravy; season to taste with salt and pepper; simmer half an hour longer. This may be used hot or cold.

Mrs. Spear.

BOILED LEG OF LAMB

WASH the lamb, put it in the kettle with enough boiling water to cover. Let it cook until tender, then add salt; the water should be boiled away to about three pints; turn out a bowlful, let the remainder of the water *simmer* away until the lamb is nicely browned (turn it often), then remove to a hot platter. Add the bowl of liquor to the fat, and thicken with flour, strain and serve.

CAPER SAUCE. — Add five tablespoonfuls of capers.

MINT SAUCE. — Add one-half cup of vinegar, a little sugar, and one-half cup of fresh chopped mint.

POT ROAST

FOUR to six pounds of the second or third cut from the rib of beef. Proceed same as above recipe for boiled lamb. Do not add more water *at last* if likely to burn, but remove to cooler part of the stove.

Mrs. Benj. H. Sanborn.

LAMB CHOPS (with green peas)

NEATLY trimmed, with bones scraped, they should then be rolled in a little melted butter and carefully broiled. When done, rub butter over them and season with pepper and salt. Slip little paper ruffles over the ends of the bones. They may be served with a centre of almost any kind of vegetable.

TOAD IN THE HOLE

1 lb. round steak   2 eggs
1 pint milk   Salt and pepper
1 cup flour

CUT the steak into dice; beat eggs very light and add to them the milk and a little salt; pour upon the flour, gradually beating till very light and smooth. Butter a two-quart dish, and in it put the meat. Season well with salt and pepper; pour over it the batter, and bake one hour in a moderate oven. Serve hot.

Mrs. Spear.

BOILED TURKEY

FILL with a few bread crumbs and one pint of oysters. Boil the turkey in a cloth.

GRAVY. — One pint of oysters mixed with the chopped giblets.

Mrs. Bacon.

CHICKEN FRICASSEE

1 chicken	1 egg
1 tablespoonful butter	1-2 teaspoonful celery salt
2 tablespoonfuls flour	1 teaspoonful lemon juice
1 cup cream or rich milk	Salt and white pepper

CUT the chicken in pieces for serving; cover with boiling water, add one teaspoonful of salt, and one-half saltspoonful white pepper. Simmer one hour, or until tender, skimming well as it comes to the boiling-point. Remove chicken and boil liquid down to one pint. Strain liquid, remove the fat, and add one cup of cream or good milk, and heat again. Melt one tablespoonful of butter in a saucepan, add two tablespoonfuls of flour; when well mixed, pour on slowly, a little at a time, the hot cream and liquid. Season to taste with salt and pepper, one-half teaspoonful of celery salt, one teaspoonful lemon juice. Beat well one egg, add a little of the hot liquid, that you may mix it smoothly with the whole.

If you wish a *white* fricassee, return the pieces of chicken to the liquid, just heat through, and serve.

For a *brown* fricassee, brown the pieces in a little butter and pour over them the sauce.

Sophia B. Horr.

BROILED CHICKENS

SELECT nice tender chickens; split them down the breast; wash very thoroughly and wipe dry; rub both sides with salt, place in baking-pan (the skin side up), cover with bits of butter, and sift over plenty of flour; turn in a little water. When nearly done, remove from oven, and place on buttered broiler, over coals not too hot. Give them a nice brown on each side. Serve with thickened gravy. In broiling this way all danger of scorching the chickens before they are done is avoided.

N. C. B.

BAKED HAM

MAKE a dough of rye meal and water, of sufficient thickness to spread well. Take a large pan and place the ham in it with the fat side down. Cover the meat with the dough about an inch thick, then turn over and completely cover it, leaving the fat side up. A twelve-pound ham will require seven hours to bake with a moderate fire. Half a ham from three to four hours.

Mrs. C. E. Shattuck.

BOILED HAM

WASH and scrape the ham, put it in a kettle with boiling water, enough to cover, keep boiling slowly until tender all through (from five to six hours for a twelve-pound ham), then remove from the fire and let stand in the kettle till cold. Remove the skin and part of the fat, put the ham on grate in a dripping-pan, stick cloves ·in the fat one inch apart. Sprinkle with cracker crumbs, bake in slow oven one hour, baste three times with sugar and water.

Mrs. B. H. Sanborn.

PRESSED CORN BEEF

TAKE a fancy brisket piece weighing six or eight pounds, put into hot water and boil eight or nine hours. Take from water with a skimmer and put into a presser. Separate the meat with a knife and fork, putting any fat pieces which may be in it in small bits all through the meat, drain off any fat or liquid remaining, put on the weights and set away to cool. In summer it will be necessary to put it on ice. It should be one solid cake or block, from which delicate slices can be cut.

Mrs. C. E. Shattuck.

MEAT PIE

TAKE cold chicken, veal, or lamb, and cut into small pieces. Over this pour milk thickened with flour, and seasoned with butter, pepper, and salt, and cook five or ten minutes.

Add rolled cracker and season with small pieces of butter. Just brown in the oven and serve hot.

Mrs. C. E. Shattuck.

SCALLOPED CHICKEN

TAKE equal parts of cold chicken, boiled rice, or macaroni. Put in layers, and cover with buttered crumbs. Bake till brown. Cold roast turkey, using stuffing and gravy, may be prepared in the same way.

Mrs. Spear.

PRESSED CHICKEN

CHOP the meat fine, season with salt, pepper, and celery salt, moisten with some of the broth. Press in a square tin, and cut in slices when cold.

Mrs. Stoddard.

PRESSED LAMB

BOIL a quarter of lamb until tender. Remove the bones. Chop a little and stir in one teaspoonful of pepper and one heaping teaspoonful of sage. The meat should be salted while boiling. After stirring well, put into an ordinary bread tin, pressing down evenly with a spoon. If prepared while hot it will slice beautifully when cold.

B. H.

A NICE BREAKFAST DISH

COOKED meat very finely chopped and nicely seasoned, warmed in the meat broth and served on hot slices of buttered toast. Send to table on a hot platter.

P. W. Dana.

A GOOD BREAKFAST DISH

2 cupfuls cold meat chopped very fine	1 tablespoonful butter
2 cupfuls mashed potatoes	2 teaspoonfuls flour
1 cupful soup stock, or milk	Salt and pepper to taste

PUT the butter into a saucepan over the fire; when it has become hot add the flour and stir the mixture until it is smooth and frothy. Now add the stock, — or milk, — and season well with salt and pepper. Stir the liquid until it boils, then add the meat, and pour all into a shallow baker. Spread the mashed potatoes over the meat and cook fifteen minutes in a moderately hot oven. Do not cover the dish. Serve immediately on taking from the oven.

Mrs. R. M. Manly.

DRIED BEEF IN CREAM

SHAVE your beef very fine; pour over it boiling water; let it stand for a few minutes; pour this off and pour on cream; let it come to a boil; if you have not cream, use milk and butter, and thicken with a little flour. Serve in covered dish. Good for breakfast with baked potatoes.

PÂTÉS

2 cups cold meat, chopped and seasoned   1 egg

BOIL the egg and mash fine, add to the meat made very fine. Put a little rich gravy in a small frypan. When very hot add the meat. Cut rounds, as for tarts, of good paste, and bake a delicate brown. Split and fill with the hot meat, or place it between two of the rounds of paste. Serve at once. Chicken, veal, or beef can be used.

Mrs. Burrill.

VEAL LOAF

3 1-2 lbs. veal, fat and lean
1 thick slice of fat pork
Chop the whole raw
6 common crackers pounded fine

2 eggs
1-2 cup of butter .
1 tablespoonful of pepper
A little clove and any herb to suit the taste

MIX all together very thoroughly. Put it into a buttered bread tin and bake two hours.

Mrs. C. E. Shattuck.

VEAL PATTY

3 lbs. fresh veal chopped
1 heaping tablespoonful salt
1 teaspoonful pepper
8 tablespoonfuls of powdered crackers

3 tablespoonfuls of milk
A piece of butter size of an egg
Nutmeg or lemon

BAKE in a loaf and slice cold.

PRESSED MEAT

TAKE about five pounds of the top of a shank of beef. Let it be fresh and clean-looking. Wash with a wet cloth. Boil until tender, usually three or four hours. Keep but little water in the kettle, watching carefully to see that it does not burn. When the meat is done, remove it to a shallow pan. Pick out all bits of bone, gristle, and skin; chop fine, season with salt, and stir into it a little of the water left in the kettle, enough to moisten it. Pack closely into a bowl or small pan, cover, placing a weight upon it, and set away in a cold place over night.

Mrs. Tucker.

RELISH FOR LUNCH OR TEA

To one full cup of coarse bread crumbs add three cups milk, a good-sized piece butter, and one cup strong (grated) cheese. Put into a pudding dish, strew bread crumbs thickly over the top, and then bits of butter, and bake twenty minutes, or till a rich brown. Thinly spread on slices of bread and butter. This makes a nice sandwich for lunch or picnic.

HORSERADISH SAUCE

CREAM one cup of butter till very light. Add two tablespoonfuls of grated horseradish, one tablespoonful thick cream. Serve on halibut steak.

M. T.

TOMATO SAUCE (for Boiled Beef or Fish)

1-2 can tomatoes	1 tablespoon chopped onion
1 cup water	1 tablespoonful butter
2 cloves	1 tablespoonful corn starch
2 allspice berries	1-2 teaspoonful salt
1 teaspoonful mixed herbs	1-2 saltspoonful pepper

PUT the tomatoes, water, and spices on to boil in a granite saucepan. Fry the onion in the butter, add the corn starch. When well mixed with the butter, stir into the tomato. Simmer ten minutes. Add salt and pepper. Strain the sauce over the boiled meat or fish.

M. T.

WHITE SAUCE

(For Croquettes and Patties or Scalloped Potatoes)

1 pint of hot milk	2 heaping tablespoonfuls flour
2 tablespoonfuls butter	1-2 teaspoonful salt

PUT the butter in a saucepan, when it is melted add the dry flour and stir quickly till well mixed. Pour in the milk, a little at a time, mixing carefully. Stir till it boils and is smooth. Add salt; some add a little white pepper, or cayenne, and celery salt.

Mrs. B. H. Sanborn

VEGETABLES

"We now come to the root of the matter."

POTATO PUFF

Cold boiled potatoes put
  through a colander
Pepper and salt

Milk, to make quite soft
1-2 teacupful butter (melted)
2 eggs (beat separately)

BAKE in buttered earthen dish.

The Eliot.

CREAMED POTATOES

CUT cold potatoes into *very thin* slices. Have ready hot milk thickened with a slight quantity of flour, and seasoned with pepper, butter, and salt. To this add potatoes, and cook five or ten minutes.

Mrs. C. E. Shattuck.

BAKED SWEET POTATOES

TAKE medium-sized potatoes, wash, and lay them on the grating in a hot oven. When half done pierce them through with a fork to let the steam out. They are then dry and mealy.

FRIED POTATOES

PARE small potatoes, cut them in halves and each half into four pieces. Put in the frying basket and cook in boiling fat ten minutes. Drain on brown paper. Sprinkle with salt. Serve with chops or steak.

Mrs. B. H. Sanborn.

SCALLOPED POTATOES

PARE and slice good potatoes. Butter a baking dish. Place a layer of the sliced potatoes in the bottom, sprinkle with salt, pepper, and flour, and strew with bits of butter. Repeat the process until the dish is sufficiently full. Pour into the dish boiling milk until it comes up to the bottom of the top layer. Bake forty minutes, or until the potatoes are soft. Excellent for lunch with cold meat.

Mrs. Tucker.

CORN FRITTERS

1 pint grated sweet corn	1 cup flour
1 cup sweet milk	A little salt

MIX and fry the same as oysters.

Mrs. Mary L. Whipple.

ARTIFICIAL OYSTERS

1 pint green corn	1 cup flour
1 pint milk	1-2 cup butter
1 egg	Salt and pepper to taste

BEAT the egg, add the milk and melted butter, salt, and pepper. Grate the corn from off the cob, stir it into the egg and butter, then add the flour.

Drop a spoonful on to the hot gridiron and fry to a light brown. Serve hot, as you would griddle cakes.

Winifred E. Badger.

CREAMED TURNIPS

WASH and pare the small white turnip, cut into half-inch dice pieces. Boil till tender in salted water. For the cream sauce, heat a pint of milk hot. Melt a large tablespoonful of butter into which a large spoonful of flour is carefully stirred with a saltspoonful of salt. Be sure there are no lumps. Pour over the hot milk, stirring all the time. When well cooked, remove from fire, drain the turnips through a colander into the dish in which they will be served, and pour the cream sauce over them.   *Anna M. Wilson.*

VEGETABLE OYSTERS

SCRAPE vegetable oysters and throw them into cold water to prevent discoloring. When you have sufficient, cut them in pieces half an inch long, and boil in just water enough to cover till tender. Drain off the water, and serve with

White Sauce

A PINT of milk, butter the size of an egg, and a little salt. Thicken with a spoonful of flour made smooth in a little cold milk.

CAULIFLOWER

CHOOSE those that are compact and of a good color. Strip off the outside leaves, wash them thoroughly, and lay them, head downwards, in a pan of cold water and salt, which will draw out all the insects. Boil them in plenty of boiling water, with a little salt, until tender. Drain and serve with white sauce.

STEWED CARROTS

CUT the carrots lengthwise, and boil till soft; then slice very thin and serve with white sauce.

TOMATO MACARONI

1 pint macaroni   1 pint canned tomato

COOK the macaroni, pour the tomato over it. Put in a piece of butter and a little salt.

Mrs. Mary L. Whipple.

WHITE SAUCE

BOIL one pint of milk or cream; put two large table-spoonfuls of butter in a granite saucepan, stir over the fire until melted and bubbling. Add two heaping table-spoonfuls of dry flour, and stir until well mixed; pour on the hot milk gradually, and stir rapidly until smooth. Season with half-teaspoonful of salt and pepper.

BAKED MACARONI

BREAK twelve sticks, cover with boiling water, cook twenty minutes; while boiling, add one tablespoonful of salt. When done, pour in a colander and drain; when the water has run off, put the macaroni in baking dish, pour over it the white sauce given above, and add the cracker crumbs, as in the rule for the scalloped fish. Slice cheese thin, or grate it on top before cooking. Bake until the crumbs are brown, about three-quarters of an hour; this is enough for six.

C. S. Flagg.

PILAF

1 cup rice	1 tablespoonful of butter
2 cups tomato	1 slice of onion
2 cups of broth, or water	

BROWN the onion in the butter, put the rice in dry and brown lightly. Stir often, in order to brown evenly. Add the tomato and broth; if water is used, a little more butter is needed. Salt and pepper to taste. Let it simmer until the rice has taken up the liquor, then cover closely and steam for an hour in an oven not too hot. Do not stir after putting in the oven.

E. Marietta Dewing.

HOMINY SERVED AS A VEGETABLE

1 cup hominy
1 cup white corn meal
2 teaspoonfuls baking powder
2 eggs

1 1-2 cups milk
Butter size of an egg, cut in
  bits over the top

BAKE three-quarters of an hour in a pudding dish, buttered.

Mrs. Burrill.

CREAM PUFFING

1 cup cold boiled hominy mashed fine
1 small teacup white corn meal
Lump of butter size of an egg, melted

2 eggs well beaten
1-2 teacup brown sugar
1 teaspoonful salt
1 large teaspoonful of Royal
  Baking Powder
1 very full teacup milk

BAKE in a greased pudding dish for one hour, or less in a hot oven. This is very nice for tea or for dinner, served as a vegetable.

Mrs. Cowan.

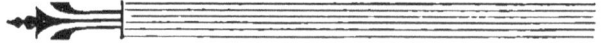

*If you wish for
Reliable Goods,
patronize those
who advertise
in this Book.*

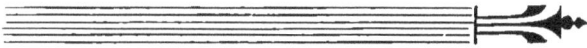

GEO. M. BOWMAN, SECY. AND SUPT.

GOLDEN GATE
PACKING CO.

PACKERS OF

EXTRA QUALITY

Canned Fruits

THESE GOODS are excelled by none, being the CHOICEST SELECTED FRUITS the season produces. Full Weight. In heavy Syrup, made from PURE White Sugar.　.·　.·　.·　.·　.·　.·

361 to 369 FOURTH STREET,
Between JULIAN and EMPIRE,

SAN JOSE, CALIFORNIA.

71

To ye Fair Dames of Wellesley.
Y^e Shattuck, Grocer,

offers ye best ingredients for ye recipes found in ye excellent cook book.

Flour — Best.   Eggs — Fresh.
  Butter — Unequalled.   Raisins — Finest.
  Canned Fruits — Choice.   Spices — Oriental.

Y^e orders receive prompt attention.

F. W. SHATTUCK . . . . WABAN SQUARE.

FANCY FLANNELS

For Ladies' house dresses, sacques, wrappers, etc. 400 pieces imported all-wool FLANNELS, in handsome plaids and stripes, always sold at 37½ cents, now at **31c.** PER YARD

SEND FOR SAMPLES.

SHEPARD, NORWELL & CO.,
BOSTON, MASS.

When I want a nice

Roast of Beef or Lamb,

or anything in fact usually kept in a first-class Market, I always go to MILTON E. SMITH, who keeps that Market in Odd Fellows' Block. If you can't be suited there, you cannot anywhere.

NATICK, MASS.

SALADS

" We may live without poetry, music, and art,
We may live without conscience, and live without heart.
We may live without friends, we may live without books,
But civilized man cannot live without cooks."

CHICKEN SALAD

THE meat of two chickens chopped, three-quarters of the same bulk of celery, the yolk of five eggs, two teaspoonfuls of mustard, one teaspoonful of pepper, one teaspoonful of salt, one-third cup of vinegar, one small bottle of olive oil, stirred gradually into the eggs, a few drops at a time. After it begins to thicken, add the other ingredients, well mixed in vinegar.

Pour over chicken and celery, and serve.

Mrs. Parritt.

LOBSTER SALAD

4 eggs	1 tablespoonful of mustard
1 tablespoonful of sugar	2 tablespoonfuls of butter
1 tablespoonful of salt	2 tablespoonfuls of vinegar

BEAT the whites of the eggs separately, and add last. Cook in a bowl set in a kettle of water, stirring until it thickens. When cold, add cream enough to make as thin as boiled custard. Add salt and red pepper to the chopped lobster and lettuce.

C. J. Hanks.

LOBSTER SALAD

(boiled fifteen minutes to a pound)

DRAIN, take out the meat, discarding the "lady," or stomach, and removing the intestine. *The liver*, called also "Tom Alley," which turns green in boiling, *should be used*, and adds much to the richness of the dish. Cut up the meat and pour over it oil and vinegar, in proportion of one tablespoonful of oil to three of vinegar. Add pepper and salt. Let stand an hour or more in ice-chest. At serving time, arrange two or three leaves of lettuce together in form of a shell, put some of the lobster (drained of oil and vinegar) in each shell, allowing a shell for each person, and putting a little mayonnaise over each.

BOILED SALAD DRESSING

1 tablespoonful of sugar	Yolks of 4 eggs
1 teaspoonful of mustard	5 tablespoonfuls salad oil
1 teaspoonful of salt	1 cup of cold milk
1 heaping teaspoonful of corn starch	1-4 cup of vinegar

MIX in the order given. Cook in a double boiler until it thickens like soft custard.

Mrs. B. H. Sanborn.

SALAD DRESSING

3 eggs	1 tablespoonful sweet oil
1 tablespoonful salt	1 teacup milk
1 tablespoonful white sugar	1 teacup vinegar
1 tablespoonful mustard	

BEAT the eggs, add salt, sugar, mustard, and oil, then add milk, and last of all the vinegar. Put in a double boiler and let it cook until it begins to thicken, *stirring constantly.*

Mrs. Peabody.

SALAD DRESSING

1 tablespoonful butter	1-2 teaspoonful mustard
1 dessertspoonful flour	1-2 teaspoonful salt
2-3 cup boiling water	1 tablespoonful sugar
Yolks of 3 eggs	2 tablespoonfuls oil
2 tablespoonfuls vinegar	A little cayenne pepper

MELT the butter in a small pan and stir in the flour until it begins to cook; then pour on the boiling water, stirring until smooth. Add the eggs well beaten, a little at a time. Place the pan in a kettle of boiling water, stirring the mixture constantly until it has thickened. Add the heated vinegar, the mustard, salt, and sugar, well mixed together, and lastly the oil.

Mrs. E. A. Jennings.

BOILED DRESSING FOR COLD SLAW

1-2 cup vinegar	1-2 saltspoonful pepper
2 teaspoonfuls sugar	1-4 cup butter
1-2 teaspoonful each of salt and mustard	1 teaspoonful of flour

MIX the first four ingredients together and allow to come to a boil. Rub the butter and flour together, and pour on it the hot vinegar. Cook five minutes and pour it over the beaten yolk of an egg.

Pauline Smith.

BOILED SALAD DRESSING

Yolks of 3 eggs	2 teaspoonfuls sugar
Whites of 3 eggs	2 teaspoonfuls melted butter
1 teaspoonful mustard	1 cup cream, or milk
2 teaspoonfuls salt	1-2 cup hot vinegar

STIR all but the beaten whites of the eggs together and cook in double boiler until like soft custard, then add the beaten whites of the eggs. Nice for lettuce, asparagus, string beans, or cauliflower, and especially so for raw chopped cabbage.

Mrs. C. E. Shattuck.

BOILED SALAD DRESSING

Yolks 4 eggs	1 tablespoonful mustard
1 cup cold milk	1 tablespoonful sugar
1 teaspoonful salt	5 tablespoonfuls salad oil

STIR eggs, mustard, sugar, salt well together. Add oil and milk, and last one-half cup vinegar. Cook in a double boiler same as custard.

Dana Hall.

CREAM SALAD DRESSING

4 eggs	1 teaspoonful salt
1 tablespoonful sugar	2 tablespoonfuls vinegar
2 tablespoonfuls butter	1 teaspoonful mustard

PUT in everything except the whites of the eggs. Cook in a bowl set in a kettle of boiling water, stirring until it thickens. Beat the whites of the eggs and add last. When cold, add cream enough to make as thin as boiled custard.

Mrs. H. H. Brown.

POTATO SALAD

CUT six large potatoes, cold boiled will do, into half-inch dice pieces, one hard-boiled egg chopped, one head of lettuce chopped with the egg. Mix well together and moisten well with home-made French dressing. Arrange in the centre of the dish and garnish with leaves of lettuce or parsley. Keep in a cool place till ready for serving, and add more of the dressing as it is brought to the table.

A. M. Wilson.

POTATO SALAD

10 potatoes	6 hard-boiled eggs, chopped fine

USE the dressing on this.

Mrs. Mary L. Whipple.

MAYONNAISE DRESSING

Yolks of 3 eggs	1 teaspoonful salt
1 cup salad oil	1 teaspoonful mustard
1-2 cup vinegar, or lemon juice	1 teaspoonful sugar
	Cayenne pepper, if liked

Mix the salt, mustard, and sugar in a soup plate. Add the yolks of eggs, and beat with a fork. When these are blended, add the oil, a little at a time. After the oil is taken up, add the vinegar or lemon juice. This should be beaten half an hour, and will be a stiff paste. If it grows too stiff, a few drops of vinegar will bring it back. Set in a cool dark place.

E. Marietta Dewing.

CABBAGE SALAD

1-2 small cabbage	2 tablespoonfuls butter, or oil
1 egg	Salt, pepper, and mustard to taste
1-2 pint vinegar	
1-2 cup sugar	

Beat egg, sugar, and spices together, and add to vinegar when boiling. Pour at once over the chopped cabbage.

C. J. Hanks.

COLD SLAW

Boil one-half cup of vinegar with two teaspoonfuls of sugar, one-half teaspoonful salt, one-half teaspoonful mustard, one-half saltspoonful of pepper.

Rub one-fourth cup of butter to a cream with one teaspoonful flour, and pour the boiling vinegar on it. Cook five minutes. Then pour it over one well-beaten egg. Mix this dressing, while hot, with one pint of cabbage shaved, or chopped very fine.

Cold slaw is delicious served with fried oysters or fish.

C. E. Cameron.

CABBAGE SALAD DRESSING

3 eggs, well beaten
3 tablespoonfuls oil, or melted
  butter
1 cup vinegar
2 tablespoonfuls sugar

1 teaspoonful each, corn
  starch, mustard, salt, and
  pepper
6 tablespoonfuls sweet cream

COOK all together but the cream, which stir in lightly with a fork before using.

Chop the solid part of a nice cabbage rather fine, then pour over it the dressing and stir thoroughly together.

A Neighbor.

CREAMED CABBAGE

1 1-2 lbs. sliced cabbage
1 cup milk
1 large spoonful flour

1 large spoonful butter
Salt and pepper

SLICE cabbage fine, and let it stand in cold water one hour, then put in boiling water and boil ten minutes; change the water, and cook slowly one hour.

Put butter in the spider, drain water from cabbage, and put in the spider. Add flour dissolved in milk, with salt and pepper to taste. Cover and simmer one-half hour.

A. M. C.

FRANK H. PORTER,

Washington St.,
Wellesley, Mass.

PLUMBER and GAS FITTER,

ALSO DEALER IN

STOVES, RANGES and FURNACES, Plumbing
Materials, and Hardware of all kinds.

TIN, SHEET IRON and PLUMBING WORK done at short notice.

Try our GOLDEN ROD BRAND of BONELESS COD FISH.

C. S. OLIVER,

Wholesale, Retail, and Commission Dealer in all kinds of

River, Lake and Ocean Fish,

Cod Liver Oil, Cape Clams, Lobsters, etc.

SOUTH AVENUE, near Depot, NATICK, MASS.

KINGSFORD'S
OSWEGO

P|URE
AND

S|ILVER
GLOSS

STARCH.

Of a rich pearly white and great strength. It never smells like inferior starches,
but is always sweet. It preserves from mildew fine laces and linens.
KINGSFORD'S OSWEGO CORN STARCH, for food purposes, is in use all
over the world. Pronounced to be equal to arrowroot in nutritious properties.

PUT UP EXPRESSLY

FOR FAMILY USE

in 3, 5, and 10 lb. pails and 10 lb. tubs; also

PURE LARD

by the tierce, barrel, half barrels and tubs; is
for sale by every first-class grocer and provi-
sion dealer—all lard rendered by us is free
from all Cotton Seed Oil, Tallow, Suet, and
other adulterations so commonly used, and
WARRANTED STRICTLY PURE. None genuine without our name stamped upon the
package.

JOHN P. SQUIRE & CO.,
BOSTON, MASS.

PIES

" Man shall not live by bread alone. "

PASTRY FOR ONE PIE

1 heaping cup of pastry flour   1-4 teaspoonful salt
1-4 teaspoonful Royal Baking   1 heaping tablespoonful lard
  Powder

Mix baking powder and salt with the flour, and rub in the lard. Mix quite stiff with cold water. Roll one half for under crust. Roll second half, spread with lard, cover thickly with flour, roll up like a jelly roll, stand on end and roll again. This secures flakiness.

Mrs. B. H. Sanborn.

TO MAKE A HEALTHFUL UNDER CRUST FOR SQUASH OR CUSTARD PIES

Spread a cold pie plate *thickly* with sweet, fresh table butter, and when done, sift over it as much finely powdered cracker crumbs as will adhere to the butter; fill and bake as usual.

With a little more care, the pulverized cracker may be used *as well* for an upper crust on fruit or mince pies. — *Proceeding with the under crust as above,* add the fruit and seasoning, and sift the powdered cracker over the top until the fruit is well covered, putting on the butter lastly, *in very thinly cut slices or shavings until the top is well covered with butter.* — The heat of the oven will do the rest.

P. W. Dana.

PUFF PASTE FOR TARTS

1 lb. flour	White of 1 egg
1-4 lb. lard	3-4 lb. butter

RUB the lard thoroughly into the flour, and mix with cold water until stiff enough to roll. Roll out quickly, put on in bits with a knife nice butter until the paste is covered. Sift on flour, roll again quickly, spread on more butter, and continue this until the butter is used.

Cut out, and, just before putting in the oven, rub over them the white of the egg well beaten.

A very hot oven is needed.

SQUASH PIE

ONE cup and a half of stewed and sifted squash, one cup of boiling milk, three-quarters of a cup of sugar, half a teaspoonful of salt, one saltspoonful of cinnamon, and one egg beaten slightly.

Mrs. Albert Jennings.

CRANBERRY PIE

ONE quart of cranberries chopped fine, two cups of sugar, one-half cup of molasses, two cups of boiling water, two tablespoonfuls of corn starch.

Enough for three pies.

Mrs. J. Moulton.

HOT CRANBERRY PIE

COVER a deep pie plate with crust, fill with fresh cranberries, then put in as much molasses as the plate will hold, cover with a top crust well tucked under.

Mrs. Stoddard.

CRANBERRY PIES

1 quart cranberries	1 1-2 cups hot water
2 cups sugar	1 tablespoonful corn starch
1-2 cup molasses	

DISSOLVE the corn starch in a little cold water, to this add one and one-half cups of hot water; put over the fire until it thickens, add one-half cup molasses, two cups sugar, pour over one quart of cranberries chopped fine.

Perforate top crust with thimble holes.

Newburyport.

APPLE PIE WITH ONE CRUST

BUTTER pie plates and fill with sliced apple. Sweeten and spice to taste. Cover and bake. When done, invert over another plate, removing the one in which it was baked.

Mrs. Tucker.

LEMON PIE

1 lemon	3 eggs
1 cup sugar	1-2 cup milk
4 tablespoonfuls powdered sugar	1 tablespoonful flour, scant
	A little salt

GRATE the yellow rind; reject the thick white skin and the seeds, cut fine the remainder of the lemon and add to the rind with the juice.

Reserve the whites of two eggs for the frosting; beat two yolks and one whole egg, then add one cup sugar, lemon, and flour, beat till very light, then add milk Bake forty minutes in a nice crust.

Whip the whites of the two eggs till very light, then add four tablespoonfuls powdered sugar. Cover the top of the pie and brown delicately.

Sophia B. Horr.

LEMON PIE

2 cups sugar	2 lemons
6 eggs	1 1-2 cups of water

BEAT the sugar and the yolks of the eggs until very light, add the rind and juice of lemons, and the water.

After the crust is ready for the filling, beat the whites to a stiff froth and add to the above.

This makes two pies.

Mrs. Pomeroy.

MINCE MEAT

2 lbs. beef boiled in very little water	1 tablespoonful cinnamon
	1 teaspoonful cloves and mace
1 lb. suet	2 nutmegs
4 lbs. apples chopped	1-2 lb. blanched almonds
3 lbs. sugar	pounded
1 lb. currants	1-4 teaspoonful almond es-
1 lb. seeded raisins	sence
1 lb. citron cut fine	1 cup grape or currant jelly
2 oranges	1 quart of fruit juice (cider,
3 lemons	grape, or currant)

MIX thoroughly, and add the beef liquor; add salt, sugar, and molasses to taste. Dredge the suet with flour and chop fine.

Bake one hour without previous cooking.

Mrs. Burrill.

RAISIN PIE

1 cup sugar	Butter the size of an egg
3 eggs	1-2 teaspoonful soda
1 1-2 cups flour	1 teaspoonful cream of tartar
1-3 cup milk	

THIS will make three layers.

For the Filling and Top.

Whites of three eggs	1 cup stoned raisins chopped
3-4 cup sugar	fine
	A little lemon or vanilla

BEAT the whites of the eggs with the sugar, and stir in the raisins and lemon.

Mrs. E. G. Fuller.

MOCK MINCE PIES

1 cup chopped raisins	1-2 cup vinegar
1 cup molasses	6 crackers rolled fine
1 cup sugar	

ALL kinds of spice, if you like.

Mrs. Hobart.

BANBERRIES

2 cups seeded and chopped raisins	1 cup powdered sugar
	1 egg, 1 lemon

GRATE outside of lemon, chop the rest fine. Make little cakes of puff paste, fill, and pinch down edges. Place on a tin, and bake a delicate brown.

LEMON PIE

FOR two pies, grated rind and juice of two lemons, one and one-half cups of cold water, one and one-half cups of sugar mixed with three heaping tablespoonfuls of flour, five eggs beaten, saving out the whites of three.

FROSTING. — To these three whites add three table-spoonfuls of powdered sugar.

Mrs. Stoddard.

LEMON PIE

INTO one pint of boiling milk stir two tablespoonfuls of corn starch, which is wet with cold milk, mix together yolks of six eggs, juice of three lemons, two cups of sugar, one tablespoonful of butter, stir all well together, cook in a double boiler, frost with the whites of eggs beaten to a stiff froth with one-half cup of sugar; put in oven to brown.

Bake the crusts separate while the filling is cooking, pricking little holes in the pastry to let the air out. This makes two large pies.

Dana Hall.

LEMON PIE

GRATE the rind of one lemon and the juice of two or three, and add one cup sugar, the yolks of three eggs, and two whole eggs, two tablespoonfuls corn starch or flour scalded in one pint milk; bake like a custard. The frosting: whites of three eggs beaten to a froth with three tablespoonfuls sugar, brown lightly. This will make two pies.

Mrs. Wilbur Hanks.

CARAMEL PIE

THREE eggs, one cup each of sugar and flour, and one teaspoonful of Dwight's Cow Brand soda. Baked in a round pie tin.

CREAM. — Boil one pint of milk, two well-beaten eggs, two spoonfuls of corn starch, and two-thirds of a cup of sugar together. When nearly done add one-half a cup of butter.

CARAMEL. — One-half a cup each of grated chocolate and water, and one cup of brown sugar. Boil till it will harden, then pour quickly over the pie in which the cream has been placed.

Miss Lucy White.

CHARLOTTE RUSSE PIE

3 eggs	1-2 cup cold water
1 1-2 cups sugar	1-2 teaspoonful Dwight's Cow
2 cups flour	Brand soda
1 teaspoonful cream tartar	

BEAT the eggs thoroughly with the sugar, add one cup flour with *even* teaspoonful cream tartar, then water with one-half teaspoonful evened of soda, and one cup flour, *no salt.* Enough for two pies.

FILLING. — Pure sweet cream, beaten until stiff,

· sweeten to taste, flavor with vanilla. Cut open pie, fill and pile some cream on top. Two cups of cream will fill two pies.

CREAM PIE

3 eggs	1 heaping teaspoonful
1 cup sugar	baking powder
2 cups flour	1-2 teaspoonful lemon
1-2 cup water	extract

BEAT the yolks and whites separately, adding one-half the sugar to each. Stir all together, and add one cup of flour. Beat five minutes. Then add the water, lemon, the other cup of flour, and the baking powder sifted with the flour.

Filling

2 eggs	3-4 cup sugar
1 pint milk	2 tablespoonfuls flour

WHEN the milk boils, add the eggs, sugar, and flour beaten together, and stir.

A. C. Withington.

CREAM PIE

3 eggs	1 cup flour
1 cup sugar	1-4 teaspoonful salt
3 tablespoonfuls water	2 teaspoonfuls yeast powder

BEAT eggs and sugar together twenty minutes, add other ingredients, beat five minutes, bake in two Washington-pie tins.

Filling

1 cup sugar	2 eggs
1-3 cup flour	1 pint milk

BOIL milk, stir in other ingredients beaten together, flavor with vanilla, and fill pies when cold.

Mrs. W. L. Russell.

✳ Fine ✳
Art Embroideries

A SPECIALTY.

R. H. STEARNS & CO.,

139 & 140 Tremont Street,

Our Stamping Books
can be seen at

2-4-6-8-10-12-14-16 Temple Place,
BOSTON.

H. E. CURRIER'S,

21 Rue Martel, PARIS.

Grove St., Wellesley.

•DYEING ᴬᴺᴰ CLEANSING•

FINELY EXECUTED AT

BARRETT'S
BOSTON · DYE · HOUSE,

H. E. CURRIER, Agent, Grove St., WELLESLEY.

Personal Attention given to

Boston Shopping

By F. H. CURRIER,

GROVE STREET, WELLESLEY.

ORDERS SOLICITED.

89

NEW STORE, GRANT'S BLOCK, Washington St., WELLESLEY.

CHOICE GROCERIES.

FRUITS, JELLIES and CANNED GOODS IN VARIETY.
GOOD ASSORTMENT OF KENNEDY'S GOODS.
NUTS AND CONFECTIONERY.
BEST GRADES OF FLOUR CONSTANTLY ON HAND.
FINE TEAS AND COFFEES A SPECIALTY.

Goods delivered in
Wellesley and vicinity. **A. B. CLARK,** WELLESLEY, MASS.

MURRAY & Water FLORIDA LANMAN'S

is the original "FLORIDA WATER,"
and must not be confounded with
the numerous trashy perfumes that
usurp its name. Remember the
name, and accept no substitute.

MURRAY & LANMAN'S
FLORIDA WATER

HAS A

DELICATE, SPRIGHTLY INDIVIDUALITY,

immediately recognized by any one
who has once used it. There is no
perfume equally applicable for the
Handkerchief, the Toilet, and the
Bath that can compare with

MURRAY & Water FLORIDA LANMAN'S

90

PUDDINGS

"Economy is a poor man's revenue,
Extravagance a rich man's ruin."

HUNTER'S PUDDING

3 brick loaves grated	1 lb. sugar
1 lb. beef suet chopped very fine	1 quart milk
	1 glass rose water
2 lbs. raisins	Large spoonful nutmeg
2 lbs. currants	Large spoonful mace
10 eggs	Large spoonful cinnamon
2 lemons, juice, grated rind	

BOIL six hours.

Sauce

1-2 lb. white sugar	A little flour
1-2 lb. butter, creamed	1 pint boiling water

COOK a few minutes. Flavor with vanilla or almond.

Miss Mary Mason.

PLUM PUDDING

1 large loaf baker's bread	1 even teaspoonful mace
2 lbs. plums	1-2 teaspoonful salt
1 lb. currants	1-2 cup molasses
1-4 lb. citron	1 large cup sugar
1 heaping teaspoonful cinnamon	1 large cup chopped suet
1 large nutmeg	3 pints milk
1-4 teaspoonful cloves	3 eggs

CUT bread in cubes one inch square, put layers in a
deep dish, alternately each ingredient. Make custard
of milk and eggs; pour over all. Stand one hour. Mix
thoroughly and bake in slow oven three hours.

Mrs. W. L. Russell.

STEAMED SUET PUDDING

1 cup molasses
1 cup cold water
1 cup chopped suet
1 cup chopped raisins   ·
1 cup currants

1 cup citron
2 to 3 cups flour
1 teaspoonful soda
Salt and spice to taste

STEAM three or four hours. Serve with hot or cold sauce, or both together.

C. J. Hanks.

BLACK PUDDING

1 teacup molasses
1-2 teacup butter
1 teacup raisins

1 teaspoonful Dwight's Cow
Brand soda
1 cup sour milk

STEAM three hours. Flour enough to make as stiff as gingerbread.

Mrs. J. E. Selfe.

BALTIMORE PUDDING

1 cup of molasses
1 cup of milk
1 cup of chopped suet, or 1-2
of butter
1 cup of stoned and chopped
raisins
3 1-2 cups of flour

1 teaspoonful of saleratus
1 teaspoonful cinnamon
1 teaspoonful of allspice and
1 of mace
1-2 teaspoonful cloves and 1-2
grated nutmeg

BEAT the molasses, suet, raisins, and spice together; then stir in the milk, in which dissolve the saleratus, then the flour. Steam five hours or more.

A. Rollins.

PLUM PUDDING

1 pound raisins
1 pound currants
1 pound suet, chopped fine
3-4 pound stale bread crumbs
1-4 pound flour

1-4 pound brown sugar
Rind of 1 lemon, grated
1-2 nutmeg
5 eggs
1-2 pound citron

MIX well all dry ingredients. Beat eggs and pour over, mixing thoroughly. To be boiled in a mould, six hours at time of making, and six more when wanted for use.

Mrs. Clements.

RAISIN PUDDING

ONE cup molasses, one cup milk, one cup raisins, one-half cup butter, two and one-half cups flour, two teaspoonfuls baking powder. Steam one hour in a tube pan.

Mrs. T. W. Willard.

ENGLISH CHRISTMAS PUDDING

ONE pound raisins, one pound currants, one pound beef suet, one pound bread crumbs, one-half pound sugar, one-half pound flour, four eggs, one-half pint milk, one-fourth pound citron, one-fourth pound candied lemon peel. Mix the dry materials, add eggs, then milk. Boil four or five hours in moulds or floured cloths plunged into boiling water.

Sauce

ONE cup frosting sugar, whites of two eggs, juice of one lemon.

Mrs. Stoddard.

VIRGINIA RICE PUDDING

4 tablespoonfuls rice	4 eggs
1 quart milk	1 lemon
Butter the size of an egg	8 tablespoonfuls powdered
Sugar to taste	sugar

WASH the rice and boil in the milk until quite soft; take it from the fire and add the butter; sweeten to taste. When cold, add the beaten yolks of the eggs and the grated rind of the lemon.

Mix into the whites the juice of the lemon and eight tablespoonfuls powdered sugar; beat till quite stiff. Put the rice in a pudding dish, with the whites smoothly over the top, place a piece of white paper over the dish, and bake a delicate brown.

Mrs. H. F. Durant.

PLAIN RICE PUDDING

ONE-HALF cup rice, one quart of milk, four tablespoonfuls sugar, and butter one-half the size of an egg, salt, and a very little nutmeg and cinnamon.
' Soak the rice in half the milk two hours, then add rest of the milk and the other things, and *bake slowly for two hours.*

P. W. Dana.

M. L. D.'S PUDDING SAUCE

THE beaten whites of one or two eggs. *When very stiff,* add the yolks and beat again — *beating or cutting them in* — then the sugar (say one or two tablespoonfuls), and *flavor to taste.* This sauce should not stand long before serving.

RICE PUDDING (without eggs)

3 tablespoonfuls raw rice	1-2 teaspoonful salt
2 cups milk	Season with cinnamon and
2 tablespoonfuls sugar	allspice

SOAK the rice in cold water three hours; pour off the water and dry the rice in a cloth. Heat the milk and pour on to the rice, boiling hot. Add the sugar, spice, and salt. Bake one hour, stirring three times. If you use raisins instead of spice, put them in at the last stirring. This pudding may be served hot, and is recommended for the winter season, when eggs are scarce.

Mrs. R. M. Manly.

BREAD AND BUTTER PUDDING (good)

LINE a pudding dish with a layer of bread, sliced, buttered, and cut in small squares. Sprinkle a few dried currants over the bread, and grate a little nutmeg over them. Cover this with a second, and, if the dish is deep, with a third layer of bread squares, currants, and nutmeg. Pour over the whole a custard made of one quart of milk (or more, till it fills the dish), four eggs, three tablespoonfuls of sugar, and a teaspoonful of vanilla. Bake as custard, and serve hot with sauce.

M. H. L.

CURATE'S PUDDING

3 eggs, weigh them in the shell   1 lemon
Same weight each of butter,   A little nutmeg (if you like)
   sugar, and flour

BEAT the butter to a cream with the sugar, add the eggs, then the flour by degrees, the peel and juice of a lemon, and a little nutmeg.

Put the batter into five cups and bake three-quarters of an hour. To be mixed two hours before baking.

Mrs. H. F. Durant.

COTTAGE PUDDING

2 eggs   1 1-2 cups flour
1 cup sugar   1 teaspoonful cream tartar
1-2 cup butter, good measure   1 teaspoonful saleratus, or
1-2 cup sweet milk   2 teaspoonfuls baking powder

BEAT very light.

Sauce

1 cup sugar   Add 2 tablespoonfuls of
1 egg, beaten light   cream, or milk
                                 Flavor to taste

BEAT very light.

C. E. Cameron.

BAKED INDIAN PUDDING

1 quart boiling milk   1-2 cup molasses
5 1-2 tablespoonfuls Indian   Salt to suit the taste
   meal

POUR the boiling milk over the meal. If you wish it jellied, stir in a little cold milk while it is baking.

A. B. Hunting.

DELICATE INDIAN PUDDING

1 quart milk	1 tablespoonful butter
2 heaping tablespoonfuls of Indian meal	3 eggs
	1 teaspoonful salt
4 tablespoonfuls sugar	

BOIL milk in double boiler. Sprinkle meal into it, stirring all the time. Cook twelve minutes. Beat together eggs, salt, sugar, and half a teaspoonful ginger. Stir butter into the meal and milk. Pour this gradually on the egg mixture. Bake slowly one hour.

Mrs. C. E. Shattuck.

INDIAN PUDDING

3 quarts milk	1 teacup molasses
2 teacups Indian meal	Butter, ginger, salt

SCALD two quarts of milk, and slowly stir in the meal, add molasses, small piece of butter, and small teaspoonful of ginger. Add the other quart of milk, and bake five or six hours.

L. T. Winsor.

BAKED INDIAN PUDDING

BOIL one quart of milk; add six tablespoonfuls of Indian meal moistened with a little milk. When it thickens, pour it into a deep dish, adding one cupful of molasses, one-half cup sugar, one teaspoonful of salt, butter one tablespoonful, tablespoonful of ginger. Now add last one pint of cold milk. Do not stir it. Bake four hours.

Dana Hall.

APPLE PUDDING

EIGHT large apples cored and filled with sugar.

Put in a deep dish and cover with a batter of milk and eggs, the same as for custard.

Mrs. Goodell.

SOFT GINGERBREAD WITH WHIPPED CREAM

ONE cup molasses, one teaspoonful Dwight's Cow Brand soda, one teaspoonful ginger, one tablespoonful of butter or lard, salt; stir all together, then pour on one-half cup of *boiling* water, two cups of flour.

Serve while hot with whipped cream, sweetened with powdered sugar, and flavored with vanilla.

Mrs. Stoddard.

FRUIT PUFFS

1 pint flour	1 pinch salt
3 teaspoonfuls baking powder	1 pint milk

PUT in buttered cups one tablespoonful of mixture, then a layer of fruit, another spoonful of the mixture. Put cups in steamer, cover tight, cook twenty minutes. Serve with cream and sugar.

Mrs. E. W. Stevens.

PAN DOWDY

1 pint flour	1 cup milk
1-4 cup sugar	1 egg
1-2 teaspoonful salt	2 teaspoonfuls butter melted
1 large teaspoonful baking powder	in two tablespoonfuls boiling water

FILL baking dish half full of sliced apples, pour over them the batter made as above, and bake.

Serve with hot sauce.

Mrs. Peabody.

DUTCH APPLE PUDDING

1 pint pastry flour	1 teaspoonful cream of tartar
1-2 teaspoonful salt	Butter size of an egg
1-2 teaspoonful Dwight's Cow Brand soda	.

MIX well. Beat one egg light, add two-thirds of a cup of milk. Pour it into the dry mixture. Stir and spread half an inch thick in a baking pan. Pare and cut into eighths four apples, stick them into the dough in rows.

Sprinkle over them two teaspoonfuls of sugar. Bake twenty minutes in a hot oven.

Pudding Sauce

1 egg	2 tablespoonfuls milk
1 cup sugar	

BEAT the egg and sugar to a froth.

Mrs. N. C. Dadmun.

APPLE DUMPLINGS

1 quart of flour	2 eggs
3 teaspoonfuls of baking	1-2 cup sugar
powder	2 quarts of apples
1 pint of milk	

MIX baking powder with the flour, beat eggs and sugar, and add to the milk, then mix thoroughly with the flour.

Cut the apples in small bits. Steam in cups. Put a little batter in the bottom of a cup well buttered, then half fill with apple, then a little more batter, till the cup is two-thirds full. Steam thirty minutes and serve with sweet rich sauce. The above recipe makes twelve common coffee-cups.

Mrs. Burrill.

ROLLED APPLE DUMPLING

MAKE a nice soda biscuit crust, roll less than a half-inch thick, spread with chopped apple, then roll and cut into pieces about two or three inches long, stand on the ends in a deep pan, putting a small piece of butter on each, and bake about one half-hour. Serve while hot, with a hard sauce.

Mrs. Stoddard.

APPLE PUDDING

Two cups of fine bread crumbs, two cups chopped apple, one cup of sugar, a little butter, and water enough to moisten it.

Put a layer of bread crumbs, then a layer of apple. Bake until apple is done.

Serve with a sweet sauce.

Mrs. James Moulton.

APPLE PUDDING

1 cup of new milk	1 teaspoonful cream tartar
2 cups of flour	1-2 teaspoonful soda
1-2 cup of butter	

PUT the apples sliced in the dish, pour over the batter, and steam two hours. Put a plate over it.

Miss Lucretia Fuller.

BROWN BETTY

1 cup bread crumbs	1 teaspoonful cinnamon
2 cups chopped apples	2 tablespoonfuls butter
1-2 cup sugar	

PUT in a layer of apples, then bread crumbs, sugar, butter in small pieces. Bake half an hour. Eat hot, with sugar and cream.

Mrs. Mary L. Whipple.

STEAMED DUMPLING

FILL a four-quart granite saucepan half full of sour apples pared and cut into quarters; add a cup of water, when thoroughly heated and nearly cooked set on a trivet to prevent burning, then add dumplings.

Take one pint of flour, two teaspoonfuls of baking powder, and half a teaspoonful of salt; wet with milk until it is a soft dough, not stiff enough to roll out.

Take a large spoon wet in water, and drop dough by spoonfuls on apple, making seven dumplings. Put cover on and steam twenty minutes. Serve with molasses, sauce, or maple syrup. These are excellent made of blueberries, adding water and sugar to berries before putting in dumplings.

Mrs. Spear.

CRANBERRY PUDDING

1-2 cup milk	Butter the size of a walnut
1-2 cup flour	1-2 teaspoonful soda
1-2 pint cranberries	1 teaspoonful cream of tartar
1-2 cup sugar	1 egg

STEAM three-quarters of an hour.

Stir the cranberries into the batter, as if they were raisins for a plum pudding.

Mrs. Edwin B. Webb.

PRUNE PUDDING

COOK half a pound of prunes in a thin syrup, and when tender remove the stones, being careful not to break the fruit. Return the stones to the syrup, and boil until it is quite thick, then strain over the fruit. When cold, beat a pint of cream to a stiff froth, and pile high over the fruit. Serve with cake or wafers.

A. L. W.

PRUNE PUDDING

ONE pound French prunes boiled and strained, to which add two-thirds cup powdered sugar, and the beaten whites of three eggs. Bake twenty minutes. Make a soft custard of one pint milk, yolks of three eggs, one-half cup sugar, flavor with vanilla.

When ready to serve use custard for a sauce for pudding.

Mrs. C. E. Shattuck.

STEAMED PEACH DUMPLINGS

FILL a deep pudding dish part full of sliced peaches, sprinkle with sugar, and add a little water. Then take one pint of flour, one heaping teaspoonful of baking powder, and a little salt. Sift four times, and mix with milk until the batter is soft enough to spread over the peaches. Steam forty minutes.

Blackberries may be used instead of peaches.

Sauce

1-2 cup butter
1 cup powdered sugar
1 egg
1-4 teaspoonful vanilla

BEAT butter and sugar to a cream, then add the egg well beaten.

Mrs. C. P. Withington.

APRICOT–TAPIOCA PUDDING

1 1-2 cups apricot marmalade
3 tablespoonfuls pearl tapioca
2-3 cup of sugar
1-2 teaspoonful salt

To prepare the marmalade : — First soak good evaporated apricots over night in cold water; then cook very slowly on the back of the range for several hours, until the fruit can easily be beaten into a smooth marmalade.

Soak the tapioca over night also; then add the salt and cook in a double boiler fifteen or twenty minutes, or until it becomes transparent. Now stir in the sugar and the marmalade, and let it simmer about ten minutes. Pour into a mould, and when cold serve with sugar and cream. This will make dessert for five.

Any kind of preserved fruit "left over" from the supper supply may take the place of apricots, but no flavor is quite so fine.

Mrs. R. M. Manly.

SPONGE PUDDING

ONE pint of milk put into double boiler. Mix one-half cup .flour, one-quarter cup of sugar, with enough cold milk to make a thin paste. Then add the boiling milk, turning on slowly, and return to boiler, and cook until it thickens, stirring all the time. Add one-quarter cup of butter, and the well-beaten yolks of five eggs, then the well-beaten whites of the eggs. Bake in an earthen pudding dish, set in pan of boiling water. Bake one-half hour exactly.

Make a sauce to eat with it, and you will find it very nice.

Mrs. S. C. Evans.

SPONGE PUDDING

1 cup of milk	3 eggs
3-4 cup of flour	1-2 teaspoonful vanilla
2 tablespoonfuls sugar	Salt
Butter half size of an egg	

PUT part of the milk in a double boiler, and while it is scalding wet the flour with the remainder and add to the hot milk, cooking until thick.

Take from the fire, and when a little cool add sugar, butter, salt, and yolks well beaten, then the whites whipped dry, and bake three-quarters of an hour in water.

To be eaten hot with a creamy sauce.

Mrs. Clough.

COCOANUT PUDDING

THREE eggs, one grated cocoanut, one and one-half cups of sugar, three and one-half cups of milk, and one-half a cup of butter. Line a deep dish with pastry, pour in the above mixture. Serve cold.

Miss Lucy White.

BAKED CHOCOLATE PUDDING

1 pint of bread crumbs	1-2 cup sugar
1 quart milk (scalded)	6 tablespoonfuls of chocolate
2 eggs	

SCALD bread and milk together, add sugar and choco-
ate, one tablespoonful of melted butter; when cool,
add eggs. To be eaten hot with cold sauce, or cold with
hot or cold sauce.

Cold Sauce.

ONE cup of sugar, one tablespoonful of butter beaten
to a cream. Beat one egg very light, and stir together.
Flavor with vanilla.

M. Brown.

ORANGE–TAPIOCA PUDDING

1-2 cup pearl tapioca	6 oranges
1 1-2 cups sugar	1 saltspoonful salt
1 quart boiling water	

WASH the tapioca, put in a double boiler with the
boiling water, salt, grated rind of three oranges, and two-
thirds of a cup of sugar. Cook until soft and transparent. Stir often while cooking. Have the oranges
sliced in a deep glass dish, sprinkle over them one cup
of sugar. When the tapioca is cooked and cold, pour it
over the oranges, and serve. Whipped cream is an
addition.

M. T.

TAPIOCA CREAM

Soak 3 tablespoonfuls tapioca till soft	Yolks 4 eggs
Scald 1 quart milk	6 tablespoonfuls sugar

ADD to tapioca, then to the milk, boil a few minutes.
Flavor, pour into a dish and cool. Beat the whites to
a stiff froth with two tablespoonfuls of sugar, and add.

E. O. K.

COCOANUT PUDDING

1 large cup bread crumbs	1-2 cup sugar
1 pint scalding milk	Butter size of butternut
1-2 cup cocoanut	Yolks of two eggs

Frosting

1-4 cup sugar	Whites of two eggs
1-2 cup cocoanut	

SPREAD on the pudding when baked, replace in the oven and brown lightly.

Mrs. N. H. Dadmun.

LIQUID SAUCE FOR PUDDING

BEAT the white and yolk of one egg separately and stiff. Mix them, and stir in a scant teacup of sugar. Set the bowl over the steam of boiling tea-kettle. Stir constantly, but slowly, until it begins to thicken. Take it off, and add the grated rind and juice of two lemons, or other flavor, and serve.

M. H. L.

PUDDING SAUCE

1 cup sugar	1-2 cup butter	1 egg

CREAM together butter and sugar, add the yolk and white of the egg beaten separately. Flavor with lemon or vanilla.

Mrs. Morrill.

PUDDING SAUCE

1 egg	1-2 cup sugar	4 tablespoonfuls milk

BEAT the white of the egg to a froth; beat the yolk and sugar together, after which add the beaten white. Heat the milk to boiling point, and pour over just before sending to the table. Flavor.

J. Peabody.

PUDDING SAUCE

1 cup sugar
1 heaping teaspoonful flour
1-4 cup butter
1 cup boiling water

1 egg
1 teaspoonful vanilla, or a
little nutmeg

MIX sugar, flour, and butter together. Just before serving, pour on the water and let it boil up once. Beat the egg and pour the liquid slowly over it, stirring all the time, and flavor. Good on any hot pudding, and on apple or peach fritters.

Mrs. Benj. H. Sanborn.

PUDDING SAUCE

1 cup sugar   1-2 cup butter

SCALD one-half pint milk, and thicken with a little flour.

Beat butter and sugar to a cream. Add to the milk, and let it come to a boil.

Miss Lucy White.

PUDDING SAUCE

1-2 cup of butter
1 cup of powdered sugar

1 egg
1-4 teaspoonful of vanilla

BEAT butter and sugar to a cream, then add the egg well beaten.

H. M. W.

COLD SAUCE

1 large cup powdered sugar   Vanilla
1-2 cup butter   Coloring

CREAM butter and sugar, color one-third red, one-third with a little melted chocolate; pile on small glass dish like a harlequin ice cream.

Mrs. W. L. Russell.

COLD SAUCE

STIR four large spoonfuls of sugar, two of butter, and the white of one egg to a cream. Flavor and serve.

Lucy White.

SYRUP FOR WAFFLES AND GRIDDLE-CAKES

2 lbs. best brown sugar   1 tablespoonful of vanilla
1 pint of water

BOIL sugar and water until it will drop thick drops from the spoon. Flavor when cool.

Mrs. Benj. H. Sanborn.

ELASTIC STARCH

The Original and Only Genuine Article of this Nature.

SINCE introducing this CELEBRATED ARTICLE, we have had a good many imitators. Like other imitators, they lack the essential qualities that make the genuine successful.

If you want to get satisfaction, use only the Original "**ELASTIC.**" It is the only Reliable and Genuine Article.

See that our Flat-Iron Trade Mark is on Every Package.

J. C. HUBINGER BROS'. CO.,

Inventors and Manufacturers,

NEW HAVEN, CONN., and KEOKUK, IOWA.

LADIES, IF YOU WOULD HAVE THE BEST,

ASK YOUR GROCER FOR

The Boston Crystal Gelatine.

BOSTON CRYSTAL GELATINE makes the most transparent jelly, and, being absolutely odorless and tasteless, requires less flavoring than any other, and is, on this account, more economical to use. It takes only about half as much of the Boston Crystal as of other kinds for any given recipe, and, the quantity being less, it will dissolve more readily. It contains no acid, and is therefore as well adapted for creams and custards as for jellies.

SMALL, OR REGULAR SIZE, 15 cents,
Making 3 pints of Jelly.

LARGE, OR DOUBLE SIZE, 20 cents,
Making 3 quarts of Jelly. Equal to 2 packages of the English Gelatine.

108

CUSTARDS AND DESSERTS

"The end crowns all."

BAKED CUSTARDS

1 pint of milk	1-2 teaspoonful salt
3 dessertspoonfuls sugar	Nutmeg or lemon flavoring
4 eggs	1-2 cup cold milk (extra)

SCALD, but not boil, the pint of milk. Beat eggs and sugar very thoroughly. To them add salt and spice (or lemon), and the half-cup of cold milk, and to this mixture the scalding milk.

Put into a pan in which is hot water six custard cups, and bake. Done when they are well browned, but not to be baked till the custard rises and falls.

H. E. C.

COFFEE CUSTARDS

1-2 pint strong coffee	4 tablespoonfuls sugar
1 pint rich milk	4 eggs; yolks

BEAT the eggs and sugar until very light. Add the boiling milk, then the coffee. Cook in the double boiler until it thickens. Serve cold with whipped cream which has been colored a pale brown with coffee.

M. T.

CARAMEL CUSTARD

1-2 cup sugar	6 eggs
3 tablespoonfuls water	1-2 teaspoonful salt
1 quart milk	1 teaspoonful vanilla

MELT the sugar, add the water, and stir into the warm milk. Beat the eggs slightly, add the salt, vanilla, and part of the milk. Strain this into the remainder of the milk, and pour into a buttered mould. Set mould in a pan of warm water, and bake thirty or forty minutes, or until firm. Serve cold with caramel sauce.

Miss Hall.

LEMON CREAM

| 1 lemon | 4 eggs |
| 2 tablespoonfuls water | 4 tablespoonfuls sugar |

BEAT yolks of eggs, add sugar, juice and rind of lemon, and water, and set on the stove. When the mixture begins to thicken, stir in the whites of the eggs, beaten to a froth, with two tablespoonfuls of sugar. Cook one or two minutes.

Mrs. Edwin B. Webb.

LEMON CREAM

DISSOLVE two tablespoonfuls of corn starch in a little water. Add the juice and grated rind of one large lemon, and one cup of sugar. On this pour two and one-half cups of boiling water. Add the yolks of three eggs. Set on the stove and cook slowly, stirring it until it thickens like custard. Remove from the fire and stir in the whites of eggs, beaten stiff, and set away to cool. It can be made the day before using.

Mrs. J. Moulton.

ORANGE FLOAT

1 pint water	2 oranges
1 cup sugar	2 eggs, whites
2 lemons	

LET sugar and water come to a boil, then stir in the juice of the lemons. Cut the oranges in slices and lay them in a glass dish, and when the lemon syrup is cold, pour it over the oranges. Beat the whites of the eggs to a stiff froth, with a little sugar, and cover the top.

Mrs. Morrill.

FLOATING ISLAND

1 quart milk	2 teaspoonfuls corn starch
4 eggs	Pinch of salt
6 tablespoonfuls sugar	Flavor with vanilla

BOIL the milk, stir in yolks of eggs, beaten with the corn starch, three tablespoonfuls sugar, and the salt. Take out a tablespoonful or two of the hot milk into your bowl before pouring out the egg mixture. Let it stand on the stove until it thickens. Pour it into baking dish. Beat the whites of the eggs to a stiff froth, and put in the rest of the sugar, and the vanilla. Pour in drops upon the pudding, and brown in the oven.

Mrs. Tucker.

SNOW PUDDING

To one small package of BOSTON CRYSTAL GELATINE add one-half cup cold water, soak half an hour, then add one cup of boiling water to dissolve the gelatine, juice of three lemons, and one cup of sugar. Beat the whites of four eggs stiff, and when the gelatine is cold, but not stiff, pour it into the egg, and beat all until it will just drop from a spoon, then put in a mould. Serve with custard made from yolks of eggs.

VELVET CREAM

1-2 box gelatine	6 tablespoonfuls white sugar
1 quart milk	1 tablespoonful flavoring
3 eggs	

PUT the gelatine and milk on the stove, add the yolks of the eggs, beaten; stir until the mixture comes to a soft custard. Beat the whites of the eggs to a froth, add the sugar and flavoring, and stir the mixture into the custard when it begins to cool. Pour into moulds. To be eaten cold, with or without sugar and cream.

Mrs. Geo. H. Robbins.

COFFEE CREAM

ONE tablespoonful of gelatine to one cup of hot water, one-fourth cup sugar. Flavor with strong coffee. When solid, serve with whipped cream, sweetened with powdered sugar, flavored with vanilla.

Mrs. Stoddard.

LEMON MERINGUE PUDDING

1 quart milk	1 cup sugar
1 pint bread crumbs	4 tablespoonfuls powdered
4 eggs	sugar
1-2 cup butter	1-2 teaspoonful salt
1 lemon	

SOAK the bread in just milk enough to cover it. Beat the yolks of the eggs and one cup of sugar together, add the juice and grated rind of the lemon. Melt the butter and stir in with the soaked bread, then put all together, stirring it well. Add the rest of the milk just before placing in the oven. Bake in a buttered dish till firm.

When done, cover with a frosting made with the whites of four eggs and four tablespoonfuls powdered sugar; return to the oven and brown slightly.

To be eaten cold.

Sophia B. Horr.

APPLE FLOAT

3 apples	4 tablespoonfuls sugar
2 eggs	1 pint milk

STEW the apples and drain till quite dry. Beat the whites of the eggs stiff, add two tablespoonfuls of sugar, and beat into the drained apple. Make a soft custard of the yolks and the milk, add two tablespoonfuls of sugar and a bit of salt. Pour the custard into a dish and lay the float on the top.

Mrs. Burrill.

CREAMED APPLES

| 1 quart apple sauce | 1 cup cream |
| 1 cup sugar | Whites of 2 eggs beaten stiff |

MIX cream, sugar, and whites of eggs together, and pour over the cold apple sauce. Time, six minutes, if the sauce is previously prepared.

A Friend.

PAINTED LADIES

CHOOSE firm, sound apples, remove the eyes, but leave the stems on, steam in a steamer till soft. Dissolve one cup of sugar in a pint of water, add three cloves and bits of lemon peel. Boil down one-half. When the apples are done lift carefully into a dish and cover the sides with jelly. Then turn the syrup into the dish, but not over the apples. Serve cold.

Pauline Smith.

ANGEL FOOD

| 1 lb. figs carefully prepared | 2 cups cold water |
| 1 cup sugar | Juice of 2 lemons |

LET cook slowly two or three hours. When cold, serve with cream.

C. J. Hanks.

CURRANT PUDDING

| 1 quart of currants fresh | 1 cup of corn starch or |
| 1-2 lb. of sugar | ground rice |

STEM the currants and put them over to boil with one pint of cold water until they are soft. Strain through a coarse cloth and boil the liquid. Dissolve the corn starch in a little cold water, and add to the liquid when boiling; boil twenty minutes, stirring constantly.

Miss Whi.

FRUIT SALAD

SLICE alternately in a glass dish layers of oranges, pineapple, bananas, grated cocoanut or the prepared cocoanut, the juice of a lemon, sprinkling each layer with sugar. If in strawberry or raspberry time a few can be used. This is best prepared the day before.

Mrs. Stoddard.

FRUIT JELLY

To one ounce package of BOSTON CRYSTAL GELATINE add one pint of cold water, place over the tea-kettle or any warm place.

To one teacup of dried apricots or other fruit, put one quart of cold water and place on back of the stove to slowly swell. When the fruit is quite soft, let it boil slowly a few minutes (never stir it and the jelly will be clear), add two cups of sugar; boil two minutes, and carefully skim the fruit into a mould.

Put the gelatine into the syrup, and just let it boil up, and pour over the fruit. When cold serve with cream and sugar.

JUDGE PETER'S PUDDING

3-4 box of Crystal Gelatine	6 figs
2 oranges	2 lemons
2 bananas	10 English walnuts

DISSOLVE the gelatine in one-half pint of cold water, then add one-half pint of boiling water, the juice of two lemons, two cups of powdered sugar.

Strain and let it stand until it begins to thicken. Stir in the fruit cut in small pieces, and turn into a mould and let it harden. Serve with whipped cream.

Mrs. Lewis M. Grant.

ORANGE TRIFLE

1 pint whipped cream	Yolks 3 eggs
1 cup powdered sugar	1-2 box gelatine
Juice 2 sweet oranges	1 cup boiling water
Grated rind of one	

MIX juice, rind, and sugar, pour the hot liquid over. Heat within a vessel of boiling water, stirring constantly to prevent curdling.

Mrs. Bacon.

ORANGE SPONGE

1-4 box of gelatine	3 oranges
1 teacup cold water	4 eggs, 1-2 pint sugar

PUT the gelatine in the water and place in a pan of hot water to dissolve, then add the juice of the oranges, the whites of the eggs beaten to a stiff froth, and the sugar. Beat about fifteen minutes and put in mould to harden. Serve with whipped cream or soft custard of the yolks beaten with two tablespoonfuls of sugar and one pint of milk.

A. C. W.

PRUNE WHIPS

1 lb. prunes	1-4 teaspoonful salt
1 small teacup sugar	1-4 teaspoonful soda
4 whites of eggs	

SOAK prunes over night in just water enough to cover them. In the morning, stone, and boil in the water in which they were soaked, until they form a thick paste, adding the sugar. When cool mix thoroughly with the whites of eggs beaten to a stiff froth, adding soda and salt.

Put in pudding dish and bake fifteen minutes, or until brown, in slow oven.

Serve cold, with cream or boiled custard.

F. E. Lord.

SNOW PUDDING

1-4 box gelatine	Yolks of 3 eggs
1-4 cup of cold water	3 tablespoonfuls sugar
1 cup boiling water	1-2 saltspoonful salt
1 cup sugar	1 pint hot milk
1-4 cup of lemon juice	1-2 teaspoonful vanilla
Whites of 3 eggs	

Soak the gelatine in the cold water fifteen minutes, or until soft. Then dissolve it in the boiling water, add the sugar and lemon juice. Stir until the sugar is dissolved. Strain into a large bowl and set away to cool. Stir occasionally. Beat the whites of the eggs to a stiff froth, and when the gelatine begins to thicken add the beaten whites, and beat all together until very light. When nearly stiff enough to drop, pour into a mould. Make a boiled custard of the yolks of the eggs, the sugar, salt, and milk, and when cool flavor with vanilla. When needed, turn the snow out on to a dish, and pour the custard around it.

The Eliot.

SNOW PUDDING

1-2 box Boston Crystal Gelatine	1 coffee-cup cold water
	1 pint boiling water
2 cups sugar, 4 eggs	Juice of 1 lemon

Soak the gelatine in the cold water for ten minutes, then pour on the boiling water, add the sugar and lemon, let stand till cool. Beat the whites of eggs to a stiff froth, add the other mixture by spoonfuls, and beat one hour; this makes the snow.

Make a soft custard of the yolks of the eggs and one quart of milk, flavor to taste. When ready to serve, pour into the dish around the snow.

Mrs. T. W. Willard.

SNOW PUDDING

ONE-THIRD package CRYSTAL GELATINE, pour upon it one pint of boiling water, place it over hot steam and stir occasionally until dissolved, which will take perhaps fifteen minutes. Add the juice of one lemon and one cup of sugar, stir well and stand away to cool; when the consistency of a soup jelly, beat two eggs to a stiff froth, then beat the jelly and froth together, and mould in any shape. Serve with soft custard.

Mrs. Albert Jennings.

RASPBERRY FLOAT

WHIP the whites of four eggs stiff, add three-fourths cup powdered sugar, beat well, then add one cup raspberry jam, and beat with a spoon or fork for twenty minutes. Pile on a glass dish and serve with cream.

Mrs. Stoddard.

FOR DESSERT

ONE glass of currant jelly well beaten, whites of two eggs beaten separately, then mix and beat together. Set away in the ice chest till wanted, then serve with soft-boiled custard.

Harriet Guardenier.

REED & BARTON,
MANUFACTURERS OF
Sterling Silver
AND
Finest Electro-Silver Plate
FOR
HOTELS, COLLEGES, AND FAMILY USE.

Factories—TAUNTON, MASS.

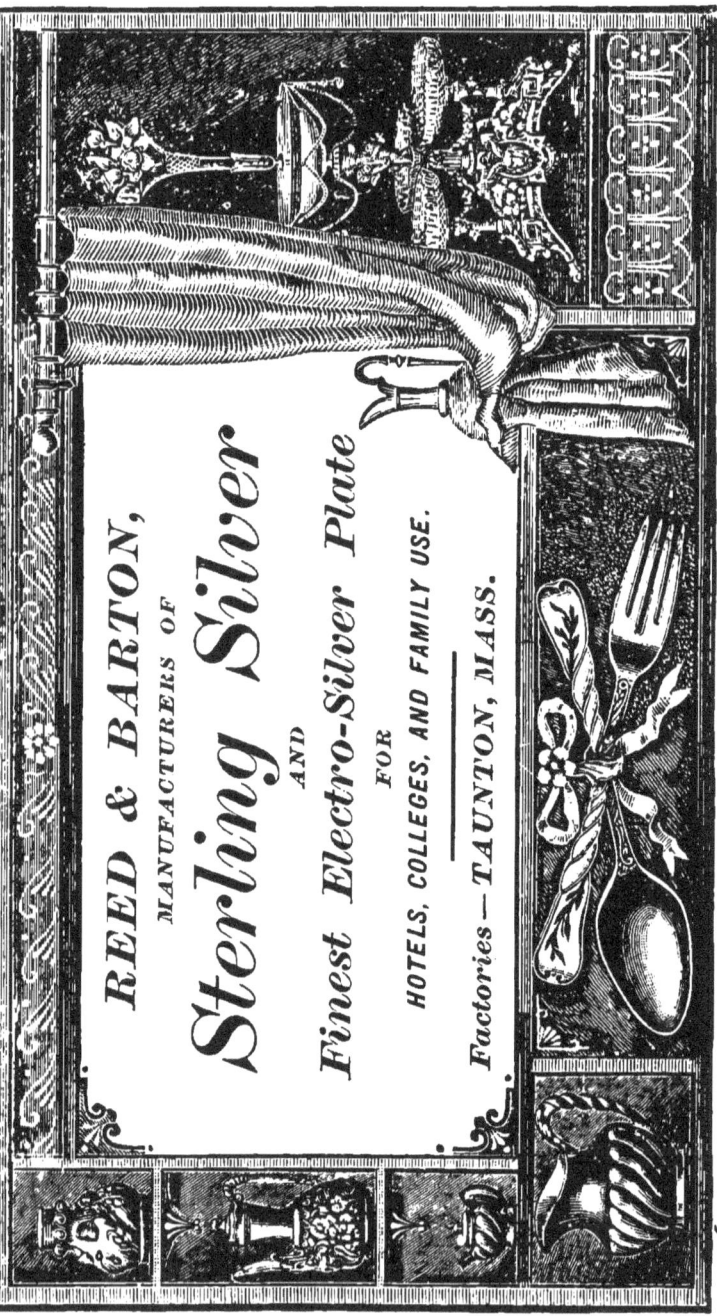

CAKE

"With weights and measures just and true,
Oven of even heat,
Well-buttered tins and quiet nerves,
Success will be complete."

"OLD TIMES" SPONGE CAKE

10 large eggs (11 if small)	1 good-sized lemon, rind
1 lb. powdered sugar	and juice
1-2 lb. flour well sifted	

BEAT the whites of the eggs very light, then the yolks. Mix together, beating the while. Then add the pound of sugar, very gradually, beating as you lightly sprinkle it in. · To this add the grated yellow rind of the lemon, then the juice. Lastly, stir in the flour. This is all-important, and must be done very gently and lightly. If stirred hard or fast while the flour is adding, or after, the cake will be dry and tough. Put immediately into a moderately brisk oven, and take out the moment it is done, which may be determined by piercing with a clean broom straw, or by the loosening of the cake from the edge of the pan. This quantity will make one small cake of four layers, or, larger, of two layers. Jelly, or an orange meringue, may be spread between the layers.

H. E. C.

EVERY-DAY SPONGE CAKE

3 eggs
1 1-2 cups sugar
2 cups flour
1-2 cup cold water

2 teaspoonfuls Royal Baking Powder
1 teaspoonful extract of lemon
1 pinch of salt

BEAT the eggs three minutes, add the sugar, beat three minutes, then one cup of flour, and beat three minutes.

Put the lemon extract into the water; the baking powder and salt into the rest of the flour. Stir into the mixture the water, then the flour.

This will make two thin loaves, baked in the bread pans twenty minutes.

Sophia B. Horr.

FALMOUTH SPONGE CAKE

6 eggs
1 3-4 cups sugar
2 cups flour

A little salt
2 large spoonfuls cold water
1 teaspoonful essence lemon

SEPARATE the eggs, beat yolks a little, add cold water and sugar, and beat well. Then beat the whites stiff, mix in, put in lemon, salt; beat up well, then stir in flour. Bake in quick oven.

Mrs. Hobart.

HOT-WATER SPONGE CAKE

6 eggs
2 cups sugar
2 coffee-cups pastry flour
1-2 cup boiling water

The grated rind of half a lemon
One teaspoonful of the juice

BEAT the yolks and sugar to a froth; also beat the whites to a stiff froth. Add the lemon to the yolks and sugar, then add the boiling water; next the whites, and last of all the flour. Mix quickly, and bake in two sheets for half an hour in a moderate oven.

H. E. C.

HOT–WATER SPONGE CAKE

4 eggs	1 heaping teaspoonful baking
2 cups sugar	powder
2 1-2 cups pastry flour	1-2 teaspoonful salt
1-2 cup hot water	

BEAT the eggs well, mix the sugar with them, put in half of the water, flour, and powder, and beat a few minutes. Then put in the rest and beat five minutes. This makes two sheets. Bake twenty minutes.

Mrs. Mary L. Whipple.

BERWICK SPONGE CAKE

3 eggs	1-2 cup cold water
1 1-2 cups sugar	1-2 teaspoonful lemon extract
2 cups flour	Pinch of salt
1 teaspoonful baking powder	

BEAT the eggs five minutes; add the sugar and beat five minutes longer, add the water, lemon extract, and the flour sifted three times with the salt and baking powder. Bake in a shallow pan, in a quick, steady oven, thirty-five minutes.

Mrs. R. M. Manly.

SPONGE CAKE

THREE eggs, beat two minutes, add one and one-half cups white sugar, and beat five minutes; one cup flour, beat two minutes, another cup of flour with one teaspoonful cream tartar stirred in, one-half cup cold water with one-half teaspoonful Dwight's Cow Brand soda, little salt and flavor. Makes two loaves.

A. B. C.

CREAM SPONGE CAKE

ONE cup sugar. Drop two eggs in a cup and fill up with cream, then beat this with the sugar. One and one-half cups flour, one and one-half teaspoonfuls Royal Baking Powder, or, if sour cream is used, a little soda.

Mrs. Wilson.

SPONGE CAKE

3 eggs	1 teaspoonful cream tartar
1 cup sugar	1 cup flour
1-2 teaspoonful soda	.

BEAT the yolks and whites separately, then beat in sugar, dissolve soda in a little water, add to the eggs and sugar, then add cream tartar to the flour, then mix all together and bake.

Mrs. J. E. Selfe.

SPONGE CAKE

BEAT the yolks of six eggs and two cups of sugar together thoroughly, add the whites of the eggs beaten to a stiff froth, beat this mixture for fifteen minutes, flavor with lemon juice or extract, stir in two cups of flour as quickly as possible, and bake immediately. Half quantity for a small loaf.

Miss Lucy White.

LADY FINGERS

| 4 eggs | 1-2 cup powdered sugar | 1 cup flour |

BEAT yolks and sugar together, add whites well beaten, then the flour. Stir as little as possible. Bake in a slow oven.

Mrs. Mary L. Whipple.

LADY FINGERS

1 cup sugar	1 pint flour
1-2 cup butter	1 teaspoonful cream of tartar
1-4 cup milk	1-2 teaspoonful soda
1 egg	

CUT into little strips, roll with your hands in sugar, and bake in a quick oven.

Mrs. N. H. Dadmun.

BOSTON MADELINES

THREE-FOURTHS cup of sugar, the same of flour, one-fourth cup of corn starch, one teaspoonful baking powder, one-third cup milk, and yolks of four eggs, flavor to taste. Bake in gem pans, one teaspoonful in each gem; use white frosting. They are very nice without any frosting, and can be baked in any shape desired.

Mrs. T. W. Willard.

JELLY ROLL

3 eggs
1 cup sugar
1 cup flour
1 teaspoonful cream tartar

1-2 teaspoonful Dwight's Cow Brand soda
1-2 teaspoonful lemon

SIFT cream tartar with the flour. Dissolve the soda in a very little water. Bake in dripping pan, spread with jelly while hot, and roll.

Wolcott, Vermont.

DELICIOUS CAKE

1 cup butter
2 cups sugar, fine granulated
1 cup milk
5 eggs, leaving out two whites

3 cups St. Louis flour
2 teaspoonfuls Royal Baking Powder

CREAM the butter. Add sugar and mix thoroughly. Add beaten yolks. Sift the baking powder into the flour. Add flour and milk to the mixture, alternately, little at a time. *Beat,* not *stir,* very thoroughly. Add beaten whites last.

Frosting

WHITE of one egg. Scant cup of powdered sugar, added gradually, and *beaten,* not *stirred.* Five table-spoonfuls grated chocolate.

C. E. Cameron.

SNOW FLAKE CAKE

1-2 cup butter	1 teaspoonful cream tartar
1 1-2 cups sugar	1-2 teaspoonful Dwight's
2 cups pastry flour	Cow Brand soda
1-4 cup milk	Juice of 1-2 lemon
5 eggs (whites only)	

BEAT the butter to a cream. Gradually add the sugar, then the lemon, and when very light the milk; next the whites of the eggs, beaten to a stiff froth, then the flour, in which the soda and cream of tartar are well mixed. Bake in sheets in a moderate oven; when nearly cool, frost.

Frosting

3 eggs (whites)	1-2 grated cocoanut
2 large cups powdered sugar	Juice of 1-2 lemon

ADD the sugar gradually to the whites, already beaten to a stiff froth, then the lemon and cocoanut. Frost the top of each loaf, or make layer cake of it by putting the sheets together.

H. E. C.

SUNSHINE CAKE

Yolks of 11 eggs	2 cups sugar
1 cup butter	1 cup milk
2 1-2 cups flour	1 teaspoonful cream tartar
1-2 teaspoonful soda	Flavor with vanilla

Mrs. S. C. Evans.

WHITE CAKE

Whites of 8 eggs	3 cups flour
2 cups sugar	1 teaspoonful cream tartar
1-2 cup butter	1-2 teaspoonful Dwight's
3-4 cup milk	Cow Brand soda

BAKE in layers; spread each layer with icing and grated cocoanut, and, when put together, cover the whole with the icing and cocoanut.

Mrs. Parritt.

RICE FLOUR CAKE

1 lb. rice flour	6 eggs
1 lb. sugar	1-4 teaspoonful Dwight's
2 3-4 cups butter	Cow Brand soda
2 3-4 cups milk	Flavor with lemon

M. M. Clark.

MOUNTAIN CAKE

1 lb. sugar	1-2 teaspoonful Dwight's
1 lb. flour	Cow Brand soda
1-2 lb. butter	1 teaspoonful cream tartar
	6 eggs

ICING to be between the layers. The cake must be baked in separate tins, same as Washington pie; when about cold, spread on the icing quite thick, and so on, making as many layers as you please.

Icing

ONE pound powdered sugar; pour over it just enough cold water to dissolve it, then take the whites of three eggs, beat them a little, but not to a froth. Add the sugar and water, put it in a bowl, place it in a vessel of boiling water, and beat the mixture. First it is thin and clear, then it begins to thicken. When quite thick, take from the fire, and beat until cold and thick enough to put on with a knife.

M. M. Clark.

BRIDE'S CAKE

1-2 cup butter	1 teaspoonful Royal Baking
1 cup sugar	Powder
Whites of 4 eggs	1 teaspoonful almond, or rose
2 tablespoonfuls milk	water
1 1-2 cups flour	

WARM the dish the cake is to be mixed in; put the butter in cold, and beat to a cream. Add the sugar slowly, and mix in the order given. Frost with white or golden frosting.

Mrs. Benj. H. Sanborn.

DELICATE CAKE

1 cup butter	1-2 cup sweet milk
2 cups sugar	4 cups flour sifted with
6 whites of eggs	2 teaspoonfuls baking powder

BEAT the butter to a cream. Whip the whites of eggs and sugar together, and add to the butter; then add the milk, and beat all together five minutes. Stir in the flour thoroughly, and bake in a quick oven one-half hour.

Winifred E. Badger.

LILY CAKE

2 cups sugar	1 cup corn starch
1 cup butter	2 cups flour
1 cup sweet milk	1 teaspoonful cream tartar
1-2 teaspoonful soda	5 eggs

CREAM together butter and sugar. Add the ingredients in the order given, and lastly the whites of the eggs, beaten to a stiff froth. Flavor with almond or vanilla, and frost with chocolate frosting.

Mrs. Morrill. '

WHITE MOUNTAIN CAKE

1-2 cup butter	1-2 teaspoonful soda
1 1-2 cups sugar	2 cups flour
2 eggs	1 teaspoonful cream of tartar
1-2 cup milk	Flavor with lemon

BAKE slowly.

Mrs. Hobart.

ONE-EGG CAKE

1-2 cup of butter	2 cups flour
1 cup sugar	1-2 teaspoonful of soda
1 egg	1 teaspoonful cream tartar
1 cup of milk	1 teaspoonful vanilla

BEAT the sugar and butter to a cream ; add the beaten egg and the milk, in which is dissolved the soda, then the flour and cream tartar mixed together. Flavor. Beat all together thoroughly.

Bake in a moderate oven.

J. Peabody.

GOLD CAKE

1-2 cup of butter	2 cups of flour
1 cup of sugar	1-2 teaspoonful cream tartar
Yolks 8 eggs	1-4 teaspoonful Dwight's Cow
1-2 cup of milk	Brand soda

Mrs. Goodell.

SILVER CAKE

2 cups sugar	3 cups flour
1-2 cup butter	1-2 teaspoonful cream tartar
Whites 8 eggs	1-4 teaspoonful soda
1-2 cup milk	

Mrs. Goodell.

FEATHER CAKE

2 cups of sugar	3 eggs
3 cups of flour	2 teaspoonfuls cream tartar
1-2 cup of butter	1 teaspoonful soda
1 small cup of milk	

A CUP of dried currants is a great addition.

Mrs. Pomeroy.

WELLESLEY CAKE

STIR together one cup white sugar, and one-half cup melted butter. Add one egg well beaten, and stir together. Into one-half cup sweet milk put one teaspoonful cream tartar and one-half teaspoonful soda, and beat to a foam. After stirring all together, add two cups flour, and flavor to taste. Bake in quick oven.

A. B. C.

COFFEE CAKE

1 cup coffee	1 teaspoonful cinnamon
1 cup molasses	1-5 teaspoonful clove
1 cup brown sugar	1-4 to 1-3 of a nutmeg
1-2 cup butter	2 teaspoonfuls baking
3 1-2 cups flour	powder
1 egg	Fruit to taste

Mary E. Horton.

COFFEE CAKE

1 cup coffee	1 teaspoonful clove
1-2 cup butter	1 teaspoonful cinnamon
1 cup sugar	1 nutmeg
1 cup molasses	1-2 lb. raisins
1 teaspoonful Dwight's Cow	4 1-2 cups flour
Brand soda	

Mrs. J. E. Selfe.

QUEEN'S CAKE

3 eggs, whites	1-2 cup milk
1 cup sugar	1 teaspoonful cream tartar
2-3 cup butter	2 cups of flour
1-2 scant teaspoonful soda	

FROST with caramel frosting.

A. M. F.

FRENCH CAKE

3 cups sugar	5 eggs
1 cup butter	1 teaspoonful cream tartar
1 cup milk	2-3 teaspoonful saleratus
4 cups flour	Flavor with lemon

THIS is sufficient for two loaves.

E. Marietta Dewing.

LADY'S CAKE

2 cups sugar	1 even teaspoonful soda
2-3 cup butter	Whites of 5 eggs
1-2 cup milk	3 cups flour
1 heaping teaspoonful cream	Flavor with almond
of tartar	

Mrs. E. G. Fuller.

DOLLY VARDEN CAKE

2 cups of sugar	1 1-2 teaspoonfuls baking
2-3 cup of butter	powder sifted three times
1 cup of milk	with 2 1-2 cups of flour
3 eggs	

BEAT the eggs thoroughly. Rub the butter and sugar to a cream, and beat well with the eggs. Add the milk and flour, and bake thirty-five minutes in a moderate oven.

Winifred E. Badger.

LEMON CAKE

1 cupful butter	Whites of 2 eggs
2 cupfuls sugar	1 1-2 teaspoonfuls baking
3 cupfuls pastry flour	powder
1 small cupful milk	Juice of 1 lemon
Yolks of 4 eggs	

BEAT the butter and sugar to a cream. Add the eggs, well beaten, next the milk, then the flour, with which the baking powder is mixed. Mix quickly, and bake in two sheets, in a moderate oven, thirty minutes. Cover with a frosting flavored with lemon.

Mrs. Mary L. Whipple.

GREEN MOUNTAIN CAKE

1 cup sugar	1-2 cup butter
Whites of 4 eggs	2 teaspoonfuls baking powder
2-3 cup sweet milk	2 1-2 cups flour

BAKE in a loaf and frost; beat the butter and sugar well together, add the flavoring, then the milk, then the flour, eggs last, beaten to a stiff froth.

Mrs. T. W. Willard.

MAGIC CAKE

1-2 cup of butter	3 tablespoonfuls milk
1 cup sugar	1 teaspoonful cream of tartar
3 eggs	1-2 teaspoonful soda
1 1-2 cups flour	Flavor with almond

Miss Lucy White.

MEASURE POUND CAKE

1 cup eggs	1 cup butter
1 1-2 cups sugar	1 1-2 cups flour

CREAM the butter, add the flour, beat thoroughly together. Beat sugar and yolks of eggs together, and the beaten whites. The more beating the better. Bake in shallow pans.

Mrs. Bacon.

ORANGE CAKE

1 1-2 cups sugar	Juice of 1 orange
Yolks 5 eggs	2 cups flour
Whites of 2	1 teaspoonful Royal Baking
1-2 cup cold water	Powder

Frosting

Grated rind 1-2 orange	Sugar enough to spread
Whites 3 eggs well beaten	nicely

RUB the grated rind into part of the sugar before adding the eggs.

Bake in three layers, and spread frosting between.

Harriet Guardenier.

ORANGE CAKE

3 cups flour	2 cups sugar
2 eggs	1 tablespoonful butter
1 cup milk	Baking powder

BAKE in jelly cake pans.

Filling

JUICE and grated rind of two oranges and one lemon, cup sugar, tablespoonful corn starch. Boil till liquid thickens, and when cold spread on cakes.

Mrs. Bacon.

ORANGE CAKE

2 cups sugar	Whites of 3 eggs
1 cup butter	1 teaspoonful cream of tartar
1 cup milk	1-2 teaspoonful soda
3 1-2 cups flour	Juice and peel of 2 oranges
Yolks of 5 eggs	

BEAT the butter and sugar to a cream.

Filling and Frosting

WHITES of two eggs, grated rind of two oranges and juice of one. Confectioner's sugar to make thick.

Mrs. N. H. Dadmun.

ORANGE CAKE

2 cups sugar	Whites 3 eggs
2 cups flour	1-2 cup water
1 teaspoonful cream of tartar	A little salt
1 teaspoonful Dwight's Cow	Juice and grated rind of
Brand saleratus	1 orange
Yolks 5 eggs	

BEAT the whites to a stiff froth, add the sugar, when thoroughly mixed add the yolks, previously beaten for five minutes; bake in five tins.

Frosting between Layers

WHITES of two eggs, juice and grated rind of one orange, sugar enough to make quite stiff.

Mrs. Albert Jennings.

CHOCOLATE CAKE

1 cup butter	5 eggs, 2 whites left out
2 cups sugar	1 teaspoonful cream tartar
3 1-2 cups flour	1-2 teaspoonful Dwight's Cow
1 cup milk	Brand soda

BEAT the butter to a cream. Add the sugar gradually, then the eggs well beaten, the milk, next the flour, in which the cream of tartar has been well mixed. Dissolve soda in a teaspoonful of the milk, add, stir quickly, and bake in two sheets for thirty minutes, in a moderate oven. Ice.

Icing

Whites of 2 eggs	6 tablespoonfuls grated choc-
1 1-2 cups of powdered	olate
sugar	1 teaspoonful of vanilla

PUT the chocolate and six tablespoonfuls of the sugar in a saucepan with two spoonfuls of hot water. Stir over a hot fire until smooth and glossy. Beat the whites to a froth and add the sugar and chocolate.

H. E. C.

CHOCOLATE CAKE

1 cup of sugar	1-2 cup butter
Whites of 2 eggs	1 1-2 cups flour
1 teaspoonful cream of tartar	1-2 cup sweet milk
1-2 teaspoonful Dwight's Cow	Flavor with vanilla
Brand soda	

RUB sugar and butter to a cream, add whites of eggs beaten stiff, then flour with cream of tartar, dissolve the soda in milk and stir into cake well. Bake in three or four layers.

Frosting

Whites of 2 eggs	1 cake German sweet choco-
Powdered sugar	late

BEAT eggs stiff, stir in chocolate grated, add sugar, not enough to make the mixture too stiff. It should not be so soft as to run. Spread the frosting between the layers and over the top.

Mrs. Albert Jennings.

CHOCOLATE CARAMEL CAKE

1 cup of butter	1 cup of corn starch
2 cups of sugar	Whites of 7 eggs
1 cup of sweet milk	3 teaspoonfuls of baking
1 1-2 cups of flour	powder in flour

CREAM butter and sugar, add the milk and flour, then the corn starch, last the eggs whipped. Bake in a dripping pan.

Caramel

ONE pound brown sugar, one-fourth pound of German chocolate, one-half cup of sweet milk, butter size of an egg, tablespoonful of vanilla.

Boil until it thickens like jelly, then spread.

Mrs. H. H. Brown.

CHOCOLATE CAKE

1 square of chocolate	2 even cups of flour
1-4 cup butter	1-2 cup milk
1 cup sugar	1-2 teaspoonful soda
2 eggs	1 teaspoonful cream of tartar

MELT the chocolate in four tablespoonfuls of water. Beat the yolks and whites of the eggs separately. Cream the butter, and add the sugar, chocolate, and yolks of the eggs, a little at a time. Mix the cream of tartar and soda with the flour and add, then the milk and whites of the eggs. Frost with chocolate frosting.

Mrs. E. A. Jennings.

CHOCOLATE CAKE

4 eggs	2 cups flour
1 1-2 cups sugar	1 teaspoonful cream tartar
1 small cup cold water	1-2 teaspoonful Dwight's soda

SIFT cream of tartar and soda with flour. Bake in round tins.

Filling

1-4 cake of Baker's chocolate	Whites of 2 eggs
1 cup sugar	1 teaspoonful vanilla

BEAT the sugar, chocolate, and eggs together, and stir into the boiling milk. Boil until thick, then add the vanilla.

Abbie A. Moulton.

CHOCOLATE CAKE

1 cup butter	1 cup of milk
2 cups sugar	1-2 teaspoonful soda
5 eggs, reserving the whites of two	3 1-2 cups flour
	1 teaspoonful cream of tartar

Frosting for this Cake

ONE cup sugar, six large spoonfuls grated chocolate, whites of two eggs.

Mrs. H. H. Brown.

CHOCOLATE CAKE

1 cup sugar	1-2 cup milk
2 eggs	1 1-2 cups flour
3 tablespoonfuls melted	1 heaping teaspoonful Royal
butter	Baking Powder

BAKE in three round tins, and put together with the frosting.

Boiled Frosting

2 cups sugar	1-2 teaspoonful vanilla
1-2 cup water	6 tablespoonfuls grated
Whites of 2 eggs, beaten stiff	chocolate

BOIL the sugar and water, without stirring, until the syrup, taken up on a skewer, will "thread," and pour over the eggs in a fine stream, beating well. Add chocolate and vanilla, and beat until thick enough to spread.

Mrs. Benj. H. Sanborn.

COCOANUT CAKE

1 1-2 cups of sugar	1 teaspoonful cream tartar
1-2 cup of butter	1-2 teaspoonful soda
1-2 cup of milk	2 cups of freshly grated
2 1-2 cups of flour	cocoanut
Whites of 4 eggs	

Miss H. H. Rollins.

COCOANUT CAKE

1 cup sugar	3 tablespoonfuls butter
Yolks of 3 eggs	1 cup sweet milk
2 cups flour	2 even teaspoonfuls cream
1 even teaspoonful soda	tartar

BAKE in four round tins. Beat the whites of eggs very light, add about one-half as much sugar as for ordinary frosting. Then Schepp's desiccated cocoanut, to thicken enough to spread nicely; put between and on top. Sprinkle on some dry cocoanut, and set away to cool.

Mrs. J. Moulton.

PUFF CAKE

3 eggs	1 1-2 cups milk
2 cups sugar	3 teaspoonfuls Royal Baking
1-2 cup butter, small cup	Powder
3 cups flour	

CREAM the butter, add sugar, then cream again; add milk, then the flour, in which the baking powder has been thoroughly stirred. Flavor with extract of almond.

Mrs. Burrill.

NUT CAKE

1 cup sugar	2 teaspoonfuls Royal Baking
1-2 cup butter	Powder
2 eggs	1 large cup walnut meat,
1-2 cup sweet milk	chopped
1 1-2 cups flour	

CREAM butter and sugar; sift baking powder with the flour; mix in the order given. Bake in one loaf; frost with white frosting, and in the frosting lay halves of walnuts.

Mrs. Benj. H. Sanborn.

MINNEHAHA CAKE

2 cugs of sugar	3 eggs
1-2 cup of butter	2 teaspoonfuls cream tartar
1 cup of milk	1 teaspoonful soda

BAKE in three jelly cake tins.

Filling

1 cup sugar	1-2 cup chopped raisins
1 egg, white only	1-2 cup currant jelly

BOIL the sugar, first adding a very little water, and pour hot upon the egg, beaten stiff, then add the other ingredients, and spread between the layers while warm. A little orange or lemon juice will improve it.

Mrs. Burrill.

ALMOND CAKE

1 cup sugar	1 teaspoonful cream tartar
1-2 cup butter	1-2 teaspoonful Dwight's soda
Whites of 2 eggs	dissolved in 1-2 cup milk
2 cups flour	Flavor with almond

Mrs. Albert Jennings.

PLAIN CAKE

1 cup sugar, 1 egg	Powder
Piece of butter size of an egg	1 cup water, or milk — water
2 teaspoonfuls Royal Baking	makes tenderer cake.

CREAM together the butter and sugar, add the egg and beat *thoroughly*, add the water (or milk), and mix the baking powder with flour enough to make moderately stiff. The *amount* of flour used depends largely on the *kind* used. You need less of patent-process than of pastry. Beat all *thoroughly* once more, and bake in a loaf, or in three layers.

Essence of any kind, or raisins, or currants, or nuts, added, makes a variety.

CHOCOLATE CREAM

The Cream

2 cups granulated (or any white) sugar   3-4 cup milk

BOIL for fifteen or twenty minutes, taking care to stir often enough to keep from burning. Remove from the fire, and flavor to taste. Cool a few minutes, and stir until it thickens and begins to look like candy. Spread on cake quickly. This is enough for three layers.

The Chocolate

CUT up one-half cake Baker's chocolate. Melt by placing dish in mouth of tea-kettle. Over each layer of cream spread layer of chocolate.

Charlotte E. Miller.

VARIETY OF FROSTINGS

WITH the cream part of the above, a variety of frostings may be made, if to the boiling milk and sugar chopped raisins, or figs, or dates, or currants, or nuts, or cocoanut be added. Nuts or fruit should not be added until the frosting is about to be removed from the fire, but cocoanut may be boiled. If you wish to frost but one loaf, only half the quantity need be used.

Charlotte E. Miller.

MAPLE SUGAR FROSTING

THREE cups maple syrup boiled to a wax, and stirred until it begins to sugar, then spread quickly. Will put three layers together.

Charlotte E. Miller.

CARAMEL CAKE

2 eggs	2 cups flour
1 cup sugar	1-2 teaspoonful soda
1-2 cup butter	1 teaspoonful cream tartar
1-2 cup milk	

BEAT whites of eggs separately; cream the yolks and butter, then beat in sugar; dissolve soda in the milk and add, also flour and cream tartar. Bake in two sheets.

Filling

2 coffee-cups of powdered sugar	2-3 cup milk
	Butter size of walnut

BOIL all ten minutes, then beat till cold and creamy, and add one teaspoonful vanilla. Spread between sheets and on top.

J. Peabody.

CORNUCOPIAS FOR LUNCH

3 eggs	Salt
1 cup sugar	1 cup flour
3 tablespoonfuls water	2 teaspoonfuls yeast powder

BEAT eggs and sugar twenty minutes; add other ingredients: beat five minutes. Bake in small round tins size of teacup saucer. When taken from the oven tie each one in form of cornucopia; just before serving, remove strings and fill with whipped cream, and a square of currant jelly in centre.

Mrs. W. L. Russell.

CHARLOTTE RUSSE

1-2 pint thick cream	Sugar to taste
2 eggs (the whites)	Lemon or vanilla, to flavor
2 teaspoonfuls gelatine	1 loaf sponge cake

WHIP the cream to a froth, also the whites of the eggs; add one cup water with the gelatine dissolved in it; sweeten to taste, and flavor.

Take a deep dish and line with small strips of sponge cake on the sides. Put a piece of white paper on the bottom of the dish, then pour in the cream. Let it remain till hardened. Turn out on a flat dish to serve.

Mrs. Morrill.

DRIED APPLE CAKE

2 cupfuls apples	5 cupfuls flour
2 cupfuls molasses	3 eggs
1 cupful sugar	2 teaspoonfuls soda
1 cupful sour milk	Cloves and cinnamon
1 cupful butter	

SOAK the apples over night. Chop, and simmer in the molasses two hours. Stir the soda into the milk, beat the eggs, butter, and sugar together, and mix all together. Bake one hour.

Mrs. Mary L. Whipple.

APPLE CAKE

1 cup butter
1 cup sugar
1 egg
1 cup dried apple
1 cup molasses
1-2 cup sour milk
2 cups flour
1 teaspoonful soda

1 teaspoonful cinnamon
1-2 teaspoonful cloves and allspice
A little salt
1-2 cup raisins, stoned, chopped, and made perfectly dry

SOAK the dried apple over night. Chop it quite fine and simmer two hours in the molasses. Let it cool. Cream the butter and add to it the sugar, beating them together thoroughly. Beat the egg till very light, and add to the butter and sugar. Then put in the apple, molasses, and milk. Sift in lightly the flour, soda, and spices. Scatter the raisins into the mixture, beat thoroughly, and bake in a moderately hot oven about three-quarters of an hour. This may be frosted or not, as is liked. This receipt will make two thin or one thick loaf.

Mrs. John Anderson.

MARBLE CAKE

White Part

1-2 cup butter
1 1-2 cups sugar
1-2 cup milk
2 1-2 cups flour

Whites of 4 eggs
1-2 teaspoonful soda
1 teaspoonful cream tartar
Flavor with lemon

Dark Part

1-2 cup butter
1 cup brown sugar
1-2 cup molasses
1-2 cup milk
2 cups flour

Yolks of 4 eggs
1-2 teaspoonful soda
1 teaspoonful cream tartar
All kinds of spice

Mrs. Albert Jennings.

MARBLED CHOCOLATE CAKE

1 cup butter	1 cup sweet milk
3 cups flour	1-2 teaspoonful soda
4 eggs	1 teaspoonful cream tartar
2 cups powdered sugar	

Mix ingredients well, then take out one and one-half cups of the mixture, and mix with it enough chocolate, previously melted in a few drops of hot water, to give a dark color, then put in pans in separate layers and bake half an hour.

Mrs. Parritt.

LEOPARD CAKE

Whites of 6 eggs	6 tablespoonfuls milk
2 cups sugar	1 teaspoonful soda
4 cups pastry flour	2 teaspoonfuls cream tartar
1 cup butter	

Sift the flour, cream of tartar, and soda together; cream the butter, add the sugar, and then add gradually the eggs, flour, and milk.

The Dark Batter

1 cup butter	1 pound raisins chopped
1 cup sugar	1 pound currants
1-2 teaspoonful cloves	1 cup molasses
1 teaspoonful cinnamon	Yolks of 6 eggs
1 nutmeg	4 cups pastry flour
1 cup citron	1 teaspoonful soda

Cream the butter, and mix the other ingredients in the order given above, adding the flour and eggs in small quantities at a time. Let the currants be well dried, and mixed with a little of the flour. Put the dark batter into two pans, and mix the light batter with it in spots. Bake two hours in a moderate oven. The flavor of this cake is improved by keeping it a few weeks.

Mrs. E. A. Jennings.

MARBLE CAKE

1-2 cup of butter
1 cup of sugar
2 eggs, yolks and whites
  beaten separately

1-2 cup of milk
1 3-4 cups pastry flour
1 teaspoonful Royal Baking
  Powder

DIVIDE the mixture into halves; to one half add

1-2 cup raisins, stoned and
  chopped
1-2 cup of currants
Small piece citron, chopped

6 English walnuts, chopped
2 tablespoonfuls molasses
1 teaspoonful mixed mace
  and cassia

PUT the dark in the centre of the pan, and the light on either side. One loaf.

Mrs. B. H. Sanborn.

NED'S CAKE

1 cup butter
2 cups sugar
5 eggs
1 cup milk
3 1-2 cups flour
2 teaspoonfuls cream tartar

1 teaspoonful soda mixed with
  flour
1 cup each walnuts, raisins,
  and citron
Extract of lemon, rose, and
  bitter almond

CREAM butter and sugar, add beaten yolks of five eggs and whites of three, reserving the whites of two for frosting. Add the other ingredients, and lastly the nuts, raisins, and citron chopped. Bake in two deep pans.

Frosting

WHITES of two eggs beaten stiff, one cup of confectioner's sugar; beat smooth.

Canterbury, Conn.

VERMONT CURRANT CAKE

1-2 cup butter
1 1-4 cups sugar
1-2 cup milk
2 eggs
2 cups flour

1-2 cup currants
1-2 teaspoonful cream tartar
1-4 teaspoonful Dwight's Cow
  Brand soda

Mrs. A. Jennings.

MARSHALL CAKE

2 1-2 cups of sugar
1 cup of butter
1 cup of milk
4 cups of flour

4 eggs
1 teaspoonful soda
1 teaspoonful cream tartar

BAKE in three shallow tins, two cakes plain; to the third add

2 tablespoonfuls of molasses
1 cup of raisins, stoned and chopped
1 cup currants

1-4 lb. citron
Cloves, cinnamon, nutmeg, etc., to suit the taste

WET this after it is baked with the white of an egg, and place between the light ones.   Frost.

Miss A. Rollins.

COLD WATER CAKE

1 cup of sugar
1-2 cup of molasses
1-4 cup of butter
1-2 cup of cold water
1-2 cup of raisins

1 egg
1-2 teaspoonful of soda
A little spice of all kinds to suit taste
1 pint of flour

Mary C. Seagrave.

TUMBLER CAKE

3 tumblers sugar
1 tumbler butter
1 tumbler sweet milk
4 eggs
5 tumblers flour

1 teaspoonful cream tartar
1-2 teaspoonful soda
1 tumbler citron
Flavor with lemon

C. J. Hanks.

AUSTIN CAKE

3 cups sugar
1 cup butter
2 eggs
2 tablespoonfuls molasses
1 1-2 cups milk

5 cups flour
1 1-2 cups chopped raisins
1 teaspoonful Royal Baking Powder
1 teaspoonful mixed spices

CREAM butter and sugar, sift baking powder and spice with the flour.   Mix in the order given, and bake in two bread pans.

Mrs. B. H. Sanborn.

EMMARY CAKE

1 cup of butter	1 tablespoonful cinnamon
2 cups of sugar, and rub both together until creamed	1 teaspoonful vanilla
	2 teaspoonfuls cloves
6 eggs, beating the two parts separately	1 teaspoonful soda
	2 teaspoonfuls cream tartar
3 pints of sifted flour	1 lb. currants
1-2 cup of molasses	1-2 lb. chopped raisins
2 cups milk	1-2 lb. citron

THIS will make three loaves of cake.

N. L.

ELECTION CAKE

1 lb. raised bread dough (2 cups)	1-3 cup warm water, or milk
	1-2 teaspoonful soda
1 cup butter	1 1-2 cups flour
1 1-2 cups sugar	1 cup raisins, stoned
4 eggs	

TAKE from your bread dough which has been raised; that which you wish to use, cut in small pieces and pour over it the milk in which the soda has been dissolved; add the sugar, and the butter, melted, but *not made hot.* Mix these well together.

Beat thoroughly the eggs and add to the mixture, also the flavoring you choose, the flour, and lastly the raisins.

I use for this cake one teaspoonful extract of lemon and half a nutmeg.

Put it in a bread pan, set it in a warm place, and let rise one and a half hours. Bake in a moderate oven the same length of time.

Sophia B. Horr.

RAISED CAKE

SET a sponge, as for bread, and to a teacupful of sponge add

1 teacupful butter	2 eggs
1 teacupful sugar	Spice, raisins, and currants

Mrs. Edwin B. Webb.

RAISED CAKE

1 egg
1 1-2 cups sugar
1-2 cup butter
1-2 cup milk
1-2 cup yeast

2 1-2 cups flour
1 cup chopped raisins
1-2 teaspoonful Dwight's soda
1 teaspoonful cream tartar
Spices of all kinds

Mrs. A. Jennings.

FRUIT CAKE

1 cup chopped pork
1 cup molasses
1 cup sugar
1-2 cup water
1-2 cup milk
1 teaspoonful saleratus

1-2 lb. raisins
1 lb. currants
1-4 lb. citron
1 egg
Flour enough, so the spoon
  will stand erect

Mrs. Albert Jennings.

FRUIT CAKE

3 cups butter
3 cups brown sugar
3 cups molasses
12 eggs
8 cups flour

2 lbs. currants
2 lbs. citron
All kinds of spices
1 tablespoonful soda
1 tablespoonful cream tartar

SIFT cream of tartar in flour, and mix soda in water.
Bake three hours.

Mrs. H. H. Brown.

FRUIT CAKE

1 cup butter
2 cups sugar
3 cups flour
3 eggs

Scant cup of milk
1 cup of chopped raisins
Citron, nutmeg, cloves, and
  spice

THE juice of an orange improves the flavor.

Mrs. Caswell.

PLAIN FRUIT CAKE

2 cups sugar
2 cups molasses
2 eggs
1 cup butter
1 cup milk
1 teaspoonful soda

1 cup stoned raisins chopped
1 cup currants
1-4 lb. citron
Spice, 1 teaspoonful each
4 cups flour

THIS makes two loaves.

F. M. F.

BLACK CAKE

1 cup butter	1 cup currants
1 cup sugar	1 cup citron
1 cup molasses	2 teaspoonfuls cloves
4 eggs	2 teaspoonfuls nutmeg
4 cups flour	2 teaspoonfuls soda
1 cup raisins	Frosting or not

CREAM the butter, add the sugar; beat the eggs to a stiff froth, add to butter and sugar; then add the molasses, then the flour, saving enough to flour fruit. Stone and chop raisins, wash and dry currants, chop citron, or, if you like, cut in fine pieces. Add spices and soda. Bake three hours in moderate oven.

H. E. C.

HARRISON CAKE

3 eggs	5 cups flour
2 cups molasses	1 teaspoonful soda
1 cup sugar	1 lb. stoned raisins
1 cup butter	Nutmeg and cinnamon
1 cup milk	

BAKE in a slow oven in two iron bread pans.

Harriet Guardenier.

HARRISON CAKE

1 1-2 cups butter	1 lb. currants
2 cups sugar	1-2 lb. citron
1 cup molasses	5 cups flour
6 eggs	1 teaspoonful soda
2 lbs. raisins	Spice

Miss Mary Mason.

QUEEN'S CAKE

1 lb. flour	1 gill of cream
1 lb. sugar	5 eggs
1-2 lb. butter	Citron
1 lb. raisins	All kinds of spice
1 lb. currants	

BAKE slowly a long time.

Mrs. C. E. Shattuck.

FRUIT CAKE

1-2 cup molasses	2 eggs
1 cup sugar	1 teaspoonful soda
1-2 cup butter	Fruit and spices
2 cups flour	

E. O. K.

FROSTING FOR ONE LARGE SHEET OF CAKE

1 egg, the white	1 tablespoonful lemon juice
1 teacupful powdered sugar	

THE egg must *not* be beaten till the sugar is added. Put the white of the egg in a shallow dish and add the sugar by degrees, beating with a spoon; when all the sugar has been used, add the lemon juice.

If the white of the egg is large, it will require a very full cup of sugar; if small, a scant cup.

This will give a smooth, clear icing that will easily harden.

Sophia B. Horr.

FROSTING FOR CAKE

WHITE of one egg beaten to a stiff froth, one cup of powdered sugar. To this add one large apple grated, and beat twenty-five minutes. Flavor with vanilla.

Mrs. S. C. Evans.

CHOCOLATE FROSTING

THREE tablespoonfuls of grated chocolate, three table-spoonfuls boiling water, one-half teaspoonful vanilla, and powdered sugar to thicken.

Mrs. Benj. H. Sanborn.

CHOCOLATE FROSTING

BEAT the whites of two eggs to a stiff froth, add one and a half cups sugar and four tablespoonfuls of melted chocolate.

Mrs. Parritt.

BOSTON CREAM CAKES

1-2 pint boiling water	5 eggs
1 cup butter	1-4 teaspoonful soda
2 cups flour	

POUR the boiling water over the butter, and while hot stir in the flour. When the whole is smooth and well scalded, set away to cool. When cold, break in the eggs. Stir until perfectly mixed, then add the soda.

Drop mixture in buttered pan, tablespoonful in a place, and bake in quick oven. When done, fill the hollow cakes with cream. For cream use:

1 pint milk	1 cup sugar
1-2 cup flour	2 eggs

STIR together and heat until of the consistency of cream. Flavor with lemon.

Mrs. Clements.

CREAM CAKES

1 cup water, 1-2 cup butter	1-4 teaspoonful Dwight's
1 cup flour	Cow Brand soda
3 eggs, yolks and whites	
beaten separately	

PUT the water and butter in a saucepan and let it come to a boil, add the flour dry, beat until smooth, and remove from the fire. When cool, add the yolks and mix well, then stir in whites. Drop in tablespoonfuls, on buttered tins, about three inches apart.

Bake from twenty to thirty minutes. Split when cool and fill with cream.

Cream for Cream Cakes

1-2 pint milk	1 tablespoonful flour
2 tablespoonfuls sugar	1 egg, a little salt

WET the flour in a little cold milk and cook in the *boiling* milk five minutes, add egg and sugar, and cook one minute. When cool flavor.

ECLAIRS

BAKE the cream cake paste in oblong pieces. When cool split and fill with same cream. Ice with *chocolate* or *vanilla* frosting.

Mrs. B. H. Sanborn.

CARAMEL FROSTING

1 cup sugar	1 square Baker's chocolate
1 tablespoonful water	scraped fine

SIMMER gently twenty minutes, being careful not to let it burn. Spread on the cake while hot.

A. Rollins.

CARAMEL FROSTING

Two cups of sugar, two-thirds cup of milk, piece of butter half the size of an egg; boil together ten minutes. Flavor and beat till cool. Melt two squares of chocolate and spread on top.

A. C. W.

GOOD GINGERBREAD

2-3 cup molasses	1 teaspoonful soda
2-3 cup sugar	1 teaspoonful cinnamon
2-3 cup butter	2 teaspoonfuls ginger
1 egg	2 1-2 cups flour
1 cup sour milk	

PUT on the back of the range where it will warm, but *not* get *hot*, a dish containing the molasses, sugar, butter, spice, and a little salt, which you can stir now and then.

When you are ready to bake your gingerbread, add one egg well beaten, the milk in which the soda has been dissolved, and then the flour.

This will make one good loaf, baked in the bread pan. Time for baking, one hour.

Sophia B. Horr.

BOSTON HARD GINGERBREAD

1 lb. butter	2 lbs. flour
1 1-2 lbs. sugar	2 tablespoonfuls ginger
5 eggs	

CREAM together the butter and sugar, beat the eggs, and then add; also ginger to taste, and flour to roll very thin.

This is the very old-fashioned recipe called *Gore Gingerbread.* If put in an air-tight tin box it will keep good for several months.

Sophia B. Horr.

PATENT GINGERBREAD

3 cups flour	1 cup milk
1 cup sugar	1 cup molasses
1 teaspoonful soda	1-2 tablespoonful cloves
1 tablespoonful cinnamon	

FRUIT if you choose.

Mrs. Bacon.

FAIRY GINGERBREAD

1 cup molasses	1 teaspoonful Dwight's Cow
1 cup sugar	Brand soda
1-2 cup butter, filled with	Ginger to taste ; pinch of salt
boiling water	Flour to mix stiff

STIR molasses, sugar, ginger, and salt together, then add soda, and while *foaming* add hot water and butter. The dough should be rolled out *very thin.*

K. L. Burrill.

HARD GINGERBREAD

1 cup of sugar	1 teaspoonful of saleratus
1 cup of butter	1 tablespoonful of ginger
1-3 cup of molasses	Flour enough to roll
1-2 cup of sour milk	

ROLL thin, and bake quickly. Cut in oblong pieces while warm.

Miss A. Rollins.

MOLASSES GINGERBREAD

2 cups molasses	1 teaspoonful cinnamon
1 cup butter	1 cup boiling water with two
Nutmeg	teaspoonfuls soda dissolved
3 1-2 cups flour	in it
1 teaspoonful cloves	

Mrs. Parritt.

HARD GINGERBREAD

1 cup of butter	1-2 teaspoonful Dwight's Cow
2 cups of sugar	Brand soda
1 egg, 3-4 cup of milk	Flour to make rather a stiff
1 teaspoonful ginger or nut-meg	dough

BEAT the butter to a cream. Add the sugar, then the well-beaten egg. Dissolve soda in the milk. Add the spice, and roll very thin.

H. E. C.

MOLASSES COOKIES

1 cup molasses	1 teaspoonful Dwight's Cow
1-2 cup sugar	Brand soda
1-2 cup lard	1 teaspoonful salt
2-3 cup cold water	1 teaspoonful ginger

BEAT together sugar and lard, add molasses, water, soda *dissolved*, ginger, and salt. Roll with as little flour as possible, cut out, and bake in rather a hot oven.

H. E. C.

COOKIES

1 cup sugar	1 teaspoonful cream of tartar
1-2 cup butter	1 scant teaspoonful soda
1 egg	Flour to roll
1-2 cup milk	

CREAM the butter and sugar, add the egg well beaten, then one cup or more of flour with one teaspoonful of cream of tartar sifted with it, then add the milk in which has been dissolved the soda. Flavor, and add flour to roll.

Mrs. H. W. F. Y.

CHOCOLATE COOKIES

2 eggs
2-3 cup butter
2 teaspoonfuls cream tartar
1 1-2 cups sugar

1-2 cake chocolate
1 teaspoonful Dwight's soda
Flour enough to roll

Mrs. Albert Jennings.

SUGAR SNAPS

1 cup sugar
2-3 cup butter
1 egg
4 tablespoonfuls milk

1-2 teaspoonful Dwight's Cow
  Brand soda
1 teaspoonful cream tartar
Lemon or vanilla
Flour to roll stiff

Mrs. L. M. Grant.

HAMLETS

Two eggs, one and one-half cups of sugar, one-half cup each of raisins and currants, two-thirds cup of butter, one teaspoonful each of cinnamon, clove, and nutmeg, one teaspoonful soda dissolved in two tablespoonfuls milk, make very stiff with flour. Take pieces of dough a little larger than English walnuts and roll into balls, placing them three inches apart in buttered pans. The hands must be well floured. These are best to stand several weeks, till moist like fruit cake.

Mrs. Stoddard.

HERMIT CAKES

1 1-2 cups sugar
1 cup butter
2 eggs
1 tablespoonful milk
1 teaspoonful Dwight's Cow
  Brand soda

1 tablespoonful cinnamon
1 tablespoonful cloves
1 tablespoonful nutmeg
1 cup currants
Flour to roll thin
Sprinkle with sugar

Mrs. N. H. Dadmun.

SPICE COOKIES

1 coffee-cup lard and butter
1 coffee-cup sugar
1 coffee-cup molasses
1-2 cup boiling hot water
1 tablespoonful ginger

1 teaspoonful cloves
1-2 teaspoonful Dwight's Cow
  Brand soda dissolved in the
  water
Flour to roll stiff

Mrs. Lewis M. Grant.

GINGER SNAPS (without butter)

2 eggs well beaten
1 cup of brown sugar
1 teaspoonful of ginger
1 cup of molasses boiled

1 teaspoonful Dwight's
Cow Brand soda
Flour to roll out

Mix in the order given, bake in a quick oven.

Mrs. B. H. Sanborn.

GINGER SNAPS

1 1-2 cups molasses
1-2 cup sugar
1 cup butter
1-2 teaspoonful salt

1 tablespoonful ginger
1 tablespoonful vinegar
1 teaspoonful Dwight's Cow
Brand soda

As much flour as can be worked in. Roll thin, bake on buttered tins.

Mrs. W. L. Russell.

VANILLA WAFERS

1 cup sugar
2-3 cup butter
1 egg
4 tablespoonfuls milk

1 teaspoonful vanilla
1-4 teaspoonful soda
1-2 teaspoonful cream tartar
Flour to roll thin

Mrs. N. H. Dadmun.

BROOKLYN FLORENTINES

Make a thin, rich paste, and line a tin. Over this spread a layer of jelly, and bake. Then beat up the whites of two eggs, and pour over the top. Over this sprinkle cocoanut or minced almonds, and powdered sugar. Put into oven and brown. When done, cut in diamonds.

Mrs. B. H. Sanborn.

CRUMMETS

1 cup sugar
3-4 cup butter
2 eggs

1-2 teaspoonful saleratus
1 cup chopped raisins
Spices of all kinds

Beat butter and sugar together, add eggs, well beaten, then spice and raisins. Mix saleratus in flour. Flour enough to roll thin like cookies.

M. Brown.

ICE CREAM AND SHERBET

*" To be good be useful ; to be useful always be making
something good."*

ICE CREAM

2 quarts milk	1 small cup flour
1 quart cream	3 cups sugar

BOIL the milk and stir in the flour wet in a little cold milk. Boil ten minutes; when cold, add cream and sugar, and flavor to taste. Strain through a fine strainer and freeze.

Mrs. Burrill.

BROOKLYN PEACH ICE CREAM

To one quart of peaches take one quart of milk, sweeten the milk *very* sweet and freeze. When frozen, stir in the peaches, which have previously been sliced and sweetened, then pack.

Mrs. Benj. H. Sanborn.

VANILLA ICE CREAM

FOR two quarts of vanilla ice cream, boil two teacupfuls of milk in a milk boiler, or in a basin set inside of a pan of water. Beat the yolks of two eggs, stir them in the boiling milk, and continue stirring until it thickens like custard. When cool, add the whites of four eggs. previously beaten to a stiff froth, and one coffee-cupful of pulverized sugar. Put on the ice. When ready for freezing, add one quart of rich cream, three teaspoonfuls extract of vanilla, and freeze.

CHOCOLATE ICE CREAM

Use the recipe given above, adding to the milk, before boiling, from two to four ounces grated chocolate.

ALMOND ICE CREAM

Use the same recipe as for vanilla ice cream, except use extract of bitter almond for flavoring.

TUTTI FRUTTI ICE CREAM

Make same as ordinary ice cream, and as soon as it begins to thicken in the freezer, add candied cherries to the proportion of about six ounces of cherries to two quarts of cream. Then cover the freezer can and turn the crank so as to mix the cherries in, and beat the cream up light, until it is frozen.   *Mrs. Benj. H. Sanborn.*

FROZEN APRICOTS

1 can apricots	1 quart water
1 large pint sugar	1 pint whipped cream

Cut the apricots into small pieces, add the sugar and water, and freeze. When nearly frozen, add the cream.

Mrs. Mary L. Whipple.

CAFÉ PARFAIT

1 pint of cream	1 cup of coffee	2-3 cup sugar

Dissolve sugar in the coffee. Whip the cream thoroughly with an egg-beater, and pour in the coffee and sugar. Turn into a mould, pack in ice and salt. Let it stand two hours. This makes a pretty dish when the juice of strawberries is used instead of the coffee. More time will be required for freezing the strawberry.

Miss Hall.

FROZEN PEACHES

| 1 can peaches | 1 quart hot water |
| 1 heaping pint sugar | 2 cups whipped cream |

BOIL the sugar and water together twelve minutes; then add the peaches, and cook twenty minutes longer. Then rub through a sieve and cool. Freeze. When nearly frozen, remove the cover and add the cream. Let stand one hour before serving. Apricots may be used instead of peaches.

Pauline Smith.

FRUIT CREAM

1-2 can apricots	3 lemons
3 bananas	3 cups sugar
3 oranges	3 cups water

PUT a purée strainer or sieve over a granite pan or bowl, and turn in the apricots and rub all but skins through. Peel bananas and sift pulp. Squeeze oranges and lemons and strain into fruit pulp, add sugar, and, when dissolved, freeze as usual.

Mrs. Spear.

MILK SHERBET

| 1 quart milk | 2 cupfuls sugar |

FREEZE. Then mix in the juice of three lemons..

Mrs. Mary L. Whipple..

STRAWBERRY or BLACKBERRY SHERBET

1 quart berries, or enough to	1 pint water
make 1 pint juice	1 lemon
1 pint sugar	

MASH berries, add sugar, and, after the sugar is dissolved, add water and lemon juice. Press through fine cheese-cloth and freeze. Vary sugar as fruit requires. All fresh fruits are improved by the addition of a lemon.

Mrs. Spear.

POMEGRANATE SHERBET

DISSOLVE as much gelatine as you can heap on a large tablespoon in boiling water. To one quart of water add one and one-half cups of sugar, and the juice of eight blood-oranges. Strain and freeze.

A. M. Wilson.

GRAPE SHERBET

2 lbs. Concord grapes	1 quart water
2 lemons	1 lb. sugar

LAY a square of cheese-cloth over a large bowl; put in washed grapes and mash with wooden masher. Squeeze out all juice and add equal amount of cold water, the lemon juice, and sugar. Use sugar enough to make quite sweet. Freeze as usual.

Mrs. Spear.

RASPBERRY SHERBET

1 tablespoonful Boston Crystal Gelatine	2 cups raspberry jam
1 quart boiling water	1 cup sugar
1 lemon	1-4 cup cold water

SOAK the gelatine in the cold water ten minutes. Add half the boiling water and the sugar. Soak the jam in half the boiling water. Mix all together, add the lemon juice. Strain and freeze.

Mrs. Benj. H. Sanborn.

LEMON SHERBET

1 tablespoonful Crystal Gelatine	1 pint sugar
1 quart water	Juice of 6 lemons

SOAK the gelatine in a little of the cold water for ten minutes, and when softened add remainder of the water, the sugar and lemon juice. Strain when all is dissolved, and then freeze.

If lemons are very juicy, five will be sufficient.

J. Peabody.

CONFECTIONERY

"Prove all; hold fast that which is good."

CREAM CANDY

2 cups sugar	1 small teaspoonful cream
1 cup water	tartar
1 teaspoonful butter	1 teaspoonful vanilla

BOIL, without stirring in the least, until it will harden in cold water. After it is taken off the stove, stir in the vanilla, and turn out on a greased platter. Begin to pull as soon as you can handle it.

Mrs. Pomeroy.

NUT CANDY

2 cups molasses, "New Orleans"	3-4 cup sugar
	Coffee-cup of walnut meats

BOIL sugar and molasses until it will harden quickly in water. Add a piece of butter and the walnut meats just before removing from the fire. Pour in shallow pans and check with knife.

Mrs. C. E. Shattuck.

VINEGAR CANDY

BOIL together for twenty minutes two cups of white sugar and one of vinegar. When done, pour into shallow pans, cool, and mark into half-inch squares, or when half cool pull, making very white candy.

Miss Lucy White.

HOREHOUND CANDY

BOIL two ounces of dried horehound in a pint and a half of water for about half an hour. Strain, and add three and a half pounds brown sugar. Boil over a hot fire until it is sufficiently hard. Pour out in flat, well-buttered tin trays, and mark into small squares with a knife as soon as it is cool enough to retain its shape.

Miss Lucy White.

MAPLE SUGAR CANDY

THIS may be made of the syrup or the sugar. In either case the best and clearest should be used. If the syrup is used, put it to boil just as you would molasses. Boil it fast until it begins to get thick. Take a little on a sauce-plate and stir ; if it *grains* quickly it is done. Remove from the fire, and stir until it commences to grain, and pour into buttered pans or small muffin tins. *English walnuts or butternuts* are an addition.

Wolcott, Vermont.

BUTTER SCOTCH

1 cupful sugar	1 tablespoonful vinegar
1 cupful molasses	A pinch of soda
1-2 cupful butter, nearly	

BOIL until done. When cold, cut into squares. Wrap in paraffine paper.

Mrs. Mary L. Whipple.

ALMOND CAKE

WHITES of five eggs, stir in sugar enough to make it stiff, with just a little pinch of flour, half a pound of almonds scalded and pounded ; drop on buttered tins, and bake in a quick oven.

Mrs. Parritt.

CREAM WALNUTS

WHITE of one egg, tablespoonful of cream, confectioner's sugar enough to make a stiff batter, then roll into fairly good-sized balls. Flavor according to taste, then take one pound English walnuts, halve them, and put one half on each side of the cream, put in a cool place to harden. *May Selfe.*

NUT CAKES

ONE pound powdered sugar, whites of six eggs beaten to a stiff froth. One and one-fourth pounds almonds pounded fine in a mortar or linen cloth. Drop on buttered tins and bake in a quick oven.

NUTS AND FRUIT GLACÉ

2 cup sugar   1 cup water

BOIL slowly, without stirring, half an hour. Dip the end of a skewer into the syrup and then into cold water. If the thread formed is brittle, the syrup is done. Set the saucepan into boiling water to keep the syrup from candying. Take the prepared nuts or fruit on the point of a large needle, dip them into the syrup, and lay on buttered plates to cool. English walnuts are very nice prepared in this way. Oranges should be divided into sections without breaking the skin.

Mrs. Benj. H. Sanborn.

CHOCOLATE CAKES

WHITES of eight eggs, one pound powdered sugar, six ounces of flour. One-half pound of sweet chocolate, grated. Beat the whites stiff, add the sugar little at a time, then chocolate, then flour. Grease the tins with *lard.* Drop the mixture in small round balls, and bake in a *very quick* oven, otherwise they become thin and hard.

CHOCOLATE PUFFS

BEAT well the whites of two eggs, then add half a pound of sugar. Scrape fine one pound and a half of chocolate, dredge with flour, mixing well. Add this to the eggs and sugar. Place upon buttered tins thin spots of powdered sugar about the size of half a dollar, pile a part of the mixture upon each spot, and sift over them fine white sugar. Bake a few minutes in a quick oven.

Mrs. Clements.

CARAMELS

1 cup Baker's chocolate	1 teaspoonful flour
2 cups molasses	Good-sized piece of butter
2 cups sugar	1 teaspoonful soda
1 cup milk	

GRATE chocolate fine. When nearly done stir in soda.

When partly cool cut in checks.

CARAMELS

1-2 cup butter	1 cup grated chocolate
2 cups milk	3 cups white sugar

PUT butter and milk on together; when they boil briskly, add the sugar; when that boils, add chocolate, and boil, stirring frequently, until it is stiff and slightly granulated, which will take half an hour or more.

F. E. Lord.

COCOANUT CARAMELS

ONE pint milk, butter size of egg, one cocoanut grated fine (or desiccated cocoanut may be used), three pounds of white sugar, two teaspoonfuls lemon, boil slowly until stiff, beat to a cream, pour in shallow pans, and when partly cold cut in squares.

Miss Lucy White.

ORIENTAL DISHES

SARMAS

1-2 cup of rice   2 lbs. beef chopped very fine

BOIL the rice, mix with the chopped beef. Add a little butter, salt and pepper to taste. Take fresh grape leaves and put them in boiling water until tender. In each leaf roll a little of the beef and rice, making small oval balls, with the ends closed. Stew them in water sufficient to cover. Put a plate on them while stewing, to keep them from floating. If made with lamb instead of beef, no butter is needed.

CHESTNUT STEW

2 quarts chestnuts   3 lbs. beef

SLIT the chestnut shells, and roast until soft. Remove the shells. Cut the beef in inch squares, and brown in butter as for hash. Add a little water, flour, butter, and salt to make a gravy. Put in the roasted chestnuts and stew for about half an hour.

QUINCE AND MEAT

TAKE two good-sized quinces to two pounds beef. Pare the quinces and cut them in slices.

Cut the beef in squares about an inch in size, and brown it in butter as for hash. Add a little water, flour, butter, and salt to make a gravy. Put the quinces in, and stew until soft.

SUMMER–SQUASH DOLMAS

TAKE one-half cup rice to two pounds beef. Chop the beef fine; boil the rice and mix with the beef. Salt and pepper to taste.

Take out the inside of the squashes and fill with the rice and meat, putting a little butter in each.

Stew till the squashes are soft. If made with lamb, no butter is needed.

These may be eaten alone or with lemon sauce.

Take the yolks of five eggs to the juice of three lemons. Beat the yolks well and stir in the lemon juice. Pour over the squash dolmas.

PILAF

Two cups broth to one cup rice. When the broth comes to boiling point put in the rice. Salt to taste.

Boil the rice soft, without stirring, until all the broth is absorbed and leaves the rice only. Eat with stewed tomatoes.

DROP CAKES

1 cup sugar	1 teaspoonful baking powder
1 cup cream	Flour enough to drop from
1 egg	spoon

TAKE one-half cup pulverized sugar and one even tablespoonful cinnamon, and mix them together. Drop the cakes into the cinnamon and sugar, and put them carefully into a greased pan. Bake as long as cookies.

Agnes M. Lord, Smyrna.

SAUCE AND PICKLES

"Mingle, mingle, mingle,
You that mingle may."

RHUBARB SAUCE

4 lbs rhubarb (wine)   2 cups sugar

CUT up the rhubarb (leave the skin on), and put into an earthen dish with the sugar. Cover tightly and cook in a moderately hot oven until soft, testing with a straw. The sauce needs to be watched, as it may become too brown, and that would spoil the flavor, which is delicious when the red rhubarb is used.

Mrs. E. P. Anderson.

CRANBERRY SAUCE

1 quart cranberries   1 pint water   1 pint sugar

BOIL cranberries in water six minutes, add sugar, boil six minutes longer.

Mrs. W. L. Russell.

CRANBERRY SAUCE

3 pints of cranberries   1 1-2 pints of sugar   1 pint water

Boil eight minutes, cool in the kettle.

Miss Lucy White.

CURRANT JELLY (Never-failing)

PICK the fruit as soon as ripe (not dead-ripe). Look over carefully, but do not remove the stems; crush a little of the fruit that it may not stick to the kettle.

Cook slowly at first, then bring to a boil and cook until soft, strain through fine cheese-cloth and boil ten minutes, and measure the juice; add an equal measure of sugar which has been thoroughly heated in the oven; boil ten minutes, skimming as it boils.

Mrs. Benj. H. Sanborn.

CURRANT JELLY

Oᴺᴇ pint of juice, one pound of sugar, put the currants into the oven to warm, then press out the juice. Stir the sugar and juice together until the sugar is thoroughly dissolved, then put on the stove and stir about fifteen minutes, not letting it boil.

Miss Lucy White.

ORANGE MARMALADE

2 1-2 dozen oranges   12 lbs. coffee-crush sugar

Pᴀʀᴇ oranges very thin, cover the parings with water and boil until tender, skim them out and cut into fine shreds, and put them back in the water with the juice and pulp of the oranges, add the sugar, and boil three-quarters of an hour; do not put in seeds or skins or white part of peel. Two and one-half dozen should weigh a little over eight pounds.

A. M. C.

PRESERVED CURRANTS

5 lbs. currants   1 lb. seeded raisins   1 teacup water

To each pound of fruit allow three-fourths of a pound of sugar.

Pick currants from the stem, put currants, sugar, and raisins all in kettle together, with one cup of water to prevent burning until sugar is dissolved, and cook ten or fifteen minutes.

L. T. Winsor.

ONE, TWO, THREE JAM

2 lbs. ripe currants	4 lbs. sugar
3 lbs. raisins	6 oranges
1 pint currant juice	

SEED the raisins and chop them. Chop rather fine the peel of four of the oranges. Cook all together till soft.

Mrs. Burrill.

SPICED TOMATO

7 lbs. peeled and sliced tomato	2 1-2 tablespoonfuls ground cloves
5 lbs. sugar (crushed)	
2 1-2 tablespoonfuls ground cinnamon	1 pint good vinegar

BOIL slowly from two to three hours. Keeps well without being sealed.

P. W. Dana.

SPICED CURRANTS

8 quarts currants (stemmed)	3 teaspoonfuls ground cinnamon
4 quarts brown sugar	
1 1-2 pints cider vinegar	2 nutmegs grated
2 teaspoonfuls ground clove	

LET the pickle come to boiling, put in the currants, and boil slowly, stirring enough to prevent burning, for two hours, or until thickened as desired. Recipe fills about eight quart cans.

Mary E. Horton.

SPICED CURRANTS

5 quarts currants	1 teaspoonful ground cloves
3 lbs. brown sugar	1 teaspoonful ground cinnamon
1 pint vinegar	

PICK currants from the stems, and boil all together three-quarters of an hour. Take out the currants, and boil the syrup a quarter of an hour longer.

L. T. Winsor.

SPICED CURRANTS

7 lbs. fruit
4 lbs. sugar
1 pint vinegar

1 tablespoonful cinnamon,
cloves, allspice

BOIL slowly two hours or more.

Mrs. C. E. Shattuck.

BLACKBERRY SYRUP

2 qts. blackberry juice
1 lb. loaf sugar
1-4 oz. cloves

1-2 oz. each of nutmeg, cinnamon, and allspice
1 cup water

PULVERIZE the spice and boil fifteen minutes.
An excellent corrective for the stomach and bowels.

Mrs. Goodell.

PICKLED QUINCES

For 2 lbs. fruit allow
1 1-2 lbs. sugar
1 quart vinegar
A little whole clove

1-3 a broken, not grated, nutmeg
A handful stick cinnamon

LET the spices and sugar boil, covered, a short time in
the vinegar, then lay in the fruit — not too much at a
time, lest some pieces get overdone and broken — cover,
watch, and as fast as tender take out each piece with
spoon and lay in jar, draining carefully from pickle.
When all are done, let the pickle become as thick as
desired, then pour over the fruit until that is well
covered.

Mary E. Horton.

RASPBERRY SHRUB

PLACE red raspberries in a stone jar, cover them with
good vinegar, let them stand over night. Next morning strain, and to one pint of juice add one pint of
sugar. Boil ten minutes, and bottle while hot.

Mrs. H. H. Brown.

RASPBERRY SHRUB

To six quarts of berries add one quart of vinegar. Let them stand twenty-four hours, then strain through cheese-cloth. To one pint juice add one pound sugar. Heat slowly, allowing it to boil five or ten minutes. When cold, bottle for use. This makes a very cooling drink by adding two tablespoonfuls of the shrub and one teaspoonful of sugar to a glass of water.

Mrs. Benj. H. Sanborn.

PEAR CHIPS

8 lbs. pears, pared and quartered	1-4 lb. preserved ginger
6 lbs. sugar	1-2 dozen lemons

LET the pears, sugar, and ginger stand over night. In the morning add sliced lemons. Cook one-half hour.

A. M. C.

SWEET PICKLE PEARS

BOIL ten pounds pears until soft; make a syrup of two pounds sugar, one quart vinegar.

Miss Mary Mason.

SWEET PICKLE PEARS

7 lbs. pears	1-2 oz whole cloves
1 qt. vinegar	1-2 oz. whole allspice
3 1-2 lbs. brown sugar	1-2 oz. stick cinnamon

REMOVE the skins from the pears and steam until tender. Put the vinegar and sugar into a saucepan, add the spices and heat. When boiling hot, pour over the pears. Let them stand twenty-four hours. Then drain off the syrup, scald, and return to jar. Repeat this once more, the last time scalding both fruit and syrup.

Mrs. C. E. Shattuck.

GRAPE KETCHUP

5 pints grapes	2 tablespoonfuls cinnamon
1 pint vinegar	1 tablespoonful cloves
2 pints brown sugar	1 teaspoonful salt
1-2 tablespoonful allspice	A little cayenne pepper

Cook the grapes until soft, and sift through a colander. Add the other ingredients, and boil until the ketchup is thick.

Mrs. E. A. Jennings.

GRAPE KETCHUP

5 lbs. grapes	1-2 teaspoonful cloves
2 1-2 lbs. sugar	1-2 teaspoonful allspice
1 teaspoonful ground cinna-	1-4 teaspoonful pepper
mon	1-4 teaspoonful salt

Boil the grapes with a little more water than enough to cover them, until quite soft. Strain or rub through a sieve to get out seeds. Add sugar and spices, and boil until sufficiently thick. Bottle and seal.

Mrs. E. P. Anderson.

SWEET CUCUMBER PICKLE

Slice cucumbers about one-fourth inch thick. The cucumbers should be gathered when about an inch and a half in diameter. After slicing them crosswise, put them in a strong brine, where they will keep, if the brine is strong enough to hold up an egg, for several months, or until cold weather makes preserving a pleasant occupation.

Soak the sliced cucumbers in cold water till the salt is out, changing the water several times. Then boil one hour in strong alum water. Then soak out the alum taste in cold water, which will require several days changing the water two or three times a day. Make a syrup, one quart good vinegar, one pint water, three pounds sugar to four pounds cucumber, cinnamon, cloves, and mace to taste. Boil the cucumbers in this syrup till it is rich, clear, and thick. Some sliced ginger preserved with it is an improvement.

Knoxville, Tenn.

TOMATO KETCHUP

WASH and slice the tomatoes, and when well cooked, sift them, and to every gallon of juice add two tablespoonfuls of table salt, two tablespoonfuls of cassia, two tablespoonfuls of ground mace, one teaspoonful of cayenne pepper, one teacup of white sugar, and boil down one-third. When nearly done, add one pint of vinegar to every gallon of tomatoes.

CHILI SAUCE

TAKE thirty ripe tomatoes, peel them, three onions, three peppers, ripe ones, chop the onions and peppers very fine. Add to the partially cooked tomatoes a tablespoonful each of allspice, cloves, cinnamon, two tablespoonfuls of salt, one cup sugar, and a quart of vinegar. Cook thoroughly. Bottle, cork, and seal.

Miss Mary Mason.

TOMATO CHOW CHOW

ONE peck tomatoes, green, sliced, six green peppers, four onions, one cup salt, stirred together, and stand over night; pour off the water, put them in a kettle with vinegar enough to cover them, one cup grated horseradish, one cup sugar, one tablespoonful clove, cinnamon, allspice. Cook until soft.

Miss Mary Mason.

CHOW CHOW

To one bushel green tomatoes chopped fine, use one teacupful salt. Let them stand over night. In the morning strain off the brine. To one gallon of tomatoes allow two quarts vinegar, two peppers, one-third teaspoonful red pepper, one-half teaspoonful black pepper, and two green peppers chopped fine, one teaspoonful each of cinnamon, cloves, and allspice, one ounce celery seed, one ounce white mustard seed, and one teacupful brown sugar. Boil till tender, and can.

Harriet Guardenier.

TO PREPARE BELL PEPPERS

TAKE out the stem and seeds, and put the peppers in a brine made from two quarts salt to about eight quarts water. Let them remain nine days in the brine, then take them out, and into each pepper put a few cloves, a little allspice and mustard seed, and some horseradish. Last of all an onion. Scald your vinegar and pour on them boiling hot.

Mrs. Martha Clark.

SPANISH PICKLE

EIGHT quarts green tomatoes, chopped and salted. Let them stand twenty-four hours, then strain off the water. Add three pints each of onions and green peppers chopped, one cup of *black* mustard seed, two tablespoonfuls each ground allspice, cloves, three tablespoonfuls ginger, one of mace, two of celery seed, one coffee-cup brown sugar. Just cover with vinegar. Some prefer to boil it ten or fifteen minutes.

Mrs. C. E. Shattuck.

CUCUMBER PICKLES

2 gallons vinegar, cold
1-4 lb. ground mustard
1-4 lb. fine salt
2 oz. white mustard seed

2 oz. whole black pepper
1 oz. whole allspice
1 oz. whole cloves
Onions, if you like

WASH the cucumbers and wipe them and throw into the mixture. Stir them occasionally. They work in a few days, and will keep a long time.

M. Brown.

▲ BUY THE BEST ▲

STICKNEY & POOR'S

PURE

MUSTARDS, SPICES, AND EXTRACTS.

ABSOLUTELY PURE.   *EXTRA QUALITY.*

POOR SPICES and EXTRACTS spoil the best recipe. By calling for the above brand you are sure to get the Best. We guarantee the quality of all goods bearing our name.

Out of Paper?

TRY OUR **B**OSTON LINEN,
BOSTON BOND,
BUNKER HILL.

Excellent in Quality, and Reasonable in price. Send 6 cents for samples.

SAMUEL WARD CO.,
(INCORPORATED)
Paper Merchants and Stationers,
49 FRANKLIN ST., BOSTON.

TO HAVE
Thriving Plants,
USE

ECLIPSE FLOWER DRESSING

Gives rich foliage and abundant bloom. Insist that your seedsman furnish *Eclipse*, or send 30 cents to manufacturers — enough for 20 plants one year.

I. P. THOMAS & SON CO., Phila., Pa.

DRINK
O&O TEA
CHOICEST IMPORTED
MOST ECONOMICAL

GET YOUR

▲ PRINTING ▲

DONE AT THE

WELLESLEY JOB PRINTING OFFICE.

WABAN BLOCK,
WELLESLEY.   S. F. KINNEY, PROPRIETOR.

W. P. BIGELOW & CO.,

TRIMMINGS, BUTTONS,
∴ ZEPHYR WOOLS,
∴ YARNS, CORSETS,
WORSTED GOODS, SMALL WARES.

56 Temple Place, BOSTON.

F. DIEHL & SON,

COAL AND WOOD,

WELLESLEY and SO. NATICK.

176

FRAGMENTS AND MISCELLANEOUS HINTS

'' Therefore, in everything, ' gather up the fragments that nothing be lost.' ''

SAVE all broken pieces and crusts of bread that can-not be used for toast, and dry them in a moderate oven. When well dried pound in a mortar and sift, and put away in a glass jar to be used in scallops, croquettes, dressings, or steamed puddings.

COLD mashed potatoes, moistened with cream, and made in cakes and browned in the spider, are a good breakfast or lunch dish.

Cold boiled potatoes made into salad, or cooked Lyon-naise, are also good for lunches.

SAVE celery tops for use in salads, in soups or stews.

Fragments of mashed turnips, not enough for another meal, are just the thing for vegetable soups ; lima beans and canned peas may be pressed through the colander and added to the soup stock.

EVERY bone should be guarded with jealous care, and is the foundation for numberless delicious soups. The ends of a rib roast, the tough end of a steak and of a mutton chop are so much addition to the wealth of your soup-kettle.

Skim carefully the surface of your soup, trim your chops and steaks, and save every fragment of fat, which should be clarified and strained and used in place of lard.

FRAGMENTS of cold roast chicken, turkey, veal, or lamb, are appetizing if made into croquettes, scallops, or finely minced and seasoned and served on toast garnished by parsley or celery tops.

WHEN rice is used as a vegetable and left over, eggs may be added with a little sprinkling of flour, and light, tender, delicate griddles may be made.

COLD boiled, baked, or even fried fish may be used for croquettes, or in cream sauce, or for scallops, and prove as attractive as in the first serving.

IRON RUST. — This may be removed by salt mixed with a little lemon juice; put in the sun; if necessary, use two applications.

HOW TO CLEAN A TEA OR COFFEE POT. — If the inside of your tea or coffee pot is black from long use, fill it with water, throw in a piece of hard soap, set it on the stove, and let it boil from half an hour to an hour.

FOR A COUGH. — Mix equal parts of lemon juice, glycerine, and pure honey. Dose: One teaspoonful three times a day.

To remove the tops of fruit jars that cannot be started by hand, dip a cloth in very hot water and apply to the outside of the cap; this will cause it to expand.

SALT water, as a lotion for weak eyes, is highly recommended by many physicians, and gives much relief where eyes have been strained by overwork.

A GARGLE of salt and vinegar, with a little cayenne pepper, will do more to disperse soreness of the throat than any other remedy of which we have heard; it will sometimes cure in a few hours.

PLACE over the tight spot of a boot a cloth wrung out of hot water. The moisture causes the leather to stretch enough to make the boot fit easily.

THE best plant for a hanging basket, or the most cheerful for winter blooming, is the common morning-glory. As a window plant for winter it is a success, as it grows freely and produces graceful flowers in abundance. Besides, the morning-glory in the house has the advantage of those grown outside, as the flowers remain open nearly the whole day.

WHEN a room is to have new paper, the old ought to be removed first. A boiler of hot water set in a room, and the doors closed for a while, will cause the paper to loosen, so that it may be taken off without difficulty. The woodwork may then be cleaned easily while the dirt is softened by the steam.

ALWAYS boil macaroni, tapioca, etc., before putting them into the soup.

A LITTLL lemon juice stewed with prunes adds flavor.

SOAK gelatine in cold water. Dissolve it in boiling water.

DRAIN everything which is fried in deep lard on light brown paper before serving.

SCALLOPED oysters taste and look better when the cracker crumbs are moistened in melted butter.

A WET strip of cotton cloth put round an apple pie before baking keeps in the juices.

To test a baked custard, put a knife blade in it; it should come out clean.

SERVE melons always ice-cold.

To PREPARE SALT FOR TABLE. — Dry the salt. To one-half teacupful salt, add one teaspoonful flour, roll out and mix thoroughly. This prevents the salt from sticking in the bottles.

To REMOVE WHITE SPOTS FROM FURNITURE. — Take equal parts of spirits of turpentine and spirits of camphor. Shake till clear, and brush over the spots with a soft sponge. If necessary, rub with a little sweet oil, or any furniture polish.

To whiten laces, place them in sour milk and let them stand in the sun.

BEEF JUICE

CHOOSE a thick cut of fine, fresh, juicy "round" steak, without fat. Broil or sear it over the coals for only a minute, or long enough to merely heat it through-out. Cut it in many places, then put it in press, which should be first warmed, and squeeze the juice out into a warm bowl or pan. Salt juice slightly. It should be served immediately, free from all fat.

VANILLA

1-8 lb. vanilla beans	**1 pint alcohol**
1 tonka bean	**1 pint water**

CUT the vanilla beans up very fine, and put them and the tonka bean in the alcohol.

Leave them for one week, shaking every day. Then add the pint of water and leave another week then, if it is settled and clear, it is ready for use.

ON THE FEEDING OF YOUNG CHILDREN

WHEN planning the meals for the family table, it will well repay every mother with young children to give special thought to the demands of their rapidly growing bodies. A mother should seek to meet her child's early physical needs with as much thoughtfulness and enthusiasm as she seeks later its moral and intellectual advancement. Indeed, a mother may well feel that in properly nourishing her child's body she is directly contributing to its higher development. Yet, nothwithstanding the interest and importance that attach to this subject, in how few families are children rightly fed! Their diet is either meagre, or they are allowed to eat like their elders. What children are to eat for breakfast, dinner, and supper should never be left to chance.

The dinner should be planned with reference to the breakfast, and the meals for to-day varied from those of yesterday. In order that children may have simple and nourishing food, it is often necessary to prepare for them special dishes. This should not be thought too much trouble or too large an expense. Even a mother who keeps no maid in the kitchen may, if she choose to make herself intelligent in these matters, easily provide a suitable diet for her children. Eating between meals should not be allowed. The eating of candy is most destructive to good digestion. If sweets are craved, a block of pure sugar may be given at dessert. This is not too severe a rule. Trial proves that children are satisfied with right living when not led astray by the weak and ignorant indulgence of their parents.

When a child first comes to the family table, a little firmness on the mother's part will be required to discourage it from asking for dishes not its own. This firmness should be exercised without hesitation. As has been said above, it is easy, with a little painstaking, to interest a young child in its own well-being. What it at first accepts in obedience to its mother becomes later the child's choice and a habit of self-control. It is most important, too, that the child be taught *how* to eat. To do this will require no small amount of supervision and patience. It must be taught first by example, and the example should be supplemented by the social and physiological reasons for eating properly. Thorough mastication of solid food must be insisted on, and milk and broths should be sipped from a spoon. Milk, when taken rapidly into the stomach, forms a hard curd difficult for the stomach to break up and digest.

Baker's crackers and baker's bread, on which so many children are largely fed, are almost the worst of foods for them, as, in addition to being deficient in nourishment, they often contain ammonia or alum, on which their lightness depends. Home-made white-flour bread is also deficient in nourishment, and should be allowed only as a change from coarse bread. Bread and crackers made from whole-wheat flour, and cornmeal bread are suitable breadstuffs for children.

Starchy foods, as rice and potato, should be given sparingly.

Thoroughly cooked crushed oats, wheat and barley, gluten and wheatena, are the best of breakfast dishes for children. A saucerful of one of the above-mentioned cereals, with coarse bread, milk, and a baked apple, makes a simple, nourishing breakfast. Plain soup, lamb, beef, or chicken, roasted or broiled, with potato and one other vegetable, such as either spinach, asparagus, squash, peas, beans, cauliflower, green corn grated, and stewed celery, may form the dinner. Fresh fish, as cod, haddock, or halibut, is nourishing and useful for variety. An egg lightly boiled, or a plain omelette, may also be used as an alternate with cereals at breakfast. The supper should consist of milk and coarse bread and butter, or the bread may be made into milk-toast. Ripe fruit may be given at breakfast and dessert. If pudding or cake is given at dessert, it must be of the most simple character. The writer believes neither puddings nor cake to be necessary for a child's present happiness or future welfare. No condiment but salt should be used. Water, if possible either filtered or spring water, should be the only drink.

The diet laid down here applies only to children of from three to four years of age and upward.[1] The mother who desires a sound physical development in her children keeps them to a plain, nourishing diet until at least maturity is reached.

FRANCES FIELD ABBOTT.

[1] This is much too generous a diet for younger children. Milk, coarse bread, cereals, broths, and eggs should form the staples of a child's diet from infancy up to three and a half years. Some fruit may also be given. In most cases underdone roast lamb, beef, and chicken, minced fine, and baked potato may be used sparingly after the age of two years has been reached.

www.ingramcontent.com/pod-product-compliance
Lightning Source LLC
Chambersburg PA
CBHW020534270326
41927CB00006B/572